RECENT EXEMPLIFICATIONS OF FALSE PHILOLOGY.

BY

FITZEDWARD HALL,

M.A., HON. D.C.L. OXON.,

FORMERLY PROFESSOR OF THE SANSKRIT LANGUAGE AND LITERATURE, AND OF INDIAN JURISPRUDENCE, IN KING'S COLLEGE, LONDON.

Hoc est erroris proprium, ut, quod cuique displicet, id quoque existimet oportere displicere aliis.—*S. August.*

Discoverers of truth are, generally, sober, modest, and humble; and, if their discoveries are less valued, by mankind, than they deserve to be, can bear the disappointment with patience and equality of temper. But hasty reasoners and confident asserters are, generally, wedded to an hypothesis, and transported with joy at their fancied acquisitions, are impatient under contradiction, and grow wild at the thoughts of a refutation.—*William Cowper.*

No doubt but ye are the people, and wisdom shall die with you.—*Job.*

NEW YORK:

SCRIBNER, ARMSTRONG, & CO.

1872.

JOHN CHILDS AND SON, PRINTERS, BUNGAY.

There is scarce any truth, but its adversaries have made it an ugly vizard, by which it 's exposed to the hate and disesteem of superficial examiners. For an opprobrious title, with vulgar believers, is as good as an argument.
Joseph Glanvill.

"I AM a woman of an unspotted reputation," protests the ancient Clelia,[1] "and know nothing I have ever done which should encourage such insolence; but here was one, the other day,—and he was dressed like a gentleman, too, —who took the liberty to name the words *lusty fellow* in my presence."

It is because this lady ventured and failed, that she is now recalled from the past. The peculiar sphere of her one recorded censure, and its miscarriage, taken conjointly with her antiquity, determine for her a memorable position, if not an importance, in literary history. Of the rabble of verbal critics, English and American, we must acknowledge her, unquestionably, as the classical prototype.

In these latter days, the propagation of our vernacular philology is, for the most part, after this wise. The criticaster, having looked for a given expression, or sense of an expression, in his dictionary, but without finding it there, or even without this preliminary toil, conceives it to be novel, unauthorized, contrary to analogy, vulgar, superfluous, or what not. Flushed with his precious discovery, he explodes it before the public. Universal shallowness wonders and applauds; and Aristarchus the Little, fired to dare fresh achievements, is certain of new weeds to wreathe with his deciduous bays.

Unless we suppose that the patron of a whim is subconscious of the real nature of his pet, it is not easy to

[1] *Spectator*, No. 276. Possibly, Clelia had been reading the pious Edward Terry, and had borrowed from him her notion of the meaning of *lusty*. See *A Voyage to East-India* (ed. 1655), p. 147.

account for the fact, that he confines himself but rarely to calm statement or argument. Defect of substantial reasons must be compensated somehow; and no compensation for it is more obvious, or is oftener called into play, than an air of impatient contempt towards those who disrelish ipsedixitism.

With thus much of preface, I proceed to give illustrations of the style and temper of philologizing characterized above. Some of these illustrations are drawn, to be sure, from the works of writers to whom we are indebted for most sagacious and valuable remarks on our language. But, the greater our obligations to such writers, the more desirable is it that their invalid judgments should be discriminated from their valid. As for mere sciolists, to subject one of their number to a strict appreciation may operate, let it be hoped, as a salutary warning.

"In our own age," says Walter Savage Landor,[1] "many, Burke among the rest, say 'by *this* means'. It would be affectation to say 'by this *mean*', in the singular; but the proper expression is 'by *these means*'."

From the time of Shakespeare downwards, there are few writers but have employed the substantive *means* as a singular;[2] and, for a long time, it was, in the use of many, convertible with *mean*.[3] Even Dr. Johnson has "*this* means",[4] though he tells us, with reference to *mean*: "It is often used in the plural, and, by some, not very grammatically, with an adjective singular." "This *mean*" is

---

[1] *Last Fruit off an Old Tree*, p. 104. Bp. Lowth, in his *Grammar*, after quoting "by this *means*" from the Bible, and "by that *means*" from Atterbury, asks: "Ought it not to be 'by *these means*', 'by *those means*'? Or 'by *this mean*', 'by *that mean*', in the singular number, as it is used by Hooker, Sidney, Shakespeare, &c.?"

[2] Addison always writes "this *means*", for the singular; and so almost everybody has written since the beginning of the last century.

[3] Capgrave, *Chronicle of England* (1464), pp. 176, 241, 258, 294, 295, 300, 352, 365. Sir Thomas Elyot, *The Governour* (1531), fol. 15, 42, 49, 70, 75, 135, 146, 150, 164 (ed. 1580). *Pasquine in a Traunce* (ed. 1566), fol. 5, 11, 13, 30, 33, 71, &c. Barnabe Riche, *Farewell to Militarie Profession* (1581), pp. 10, 47, 62, 101, 116, 145, &c. (ed. 1846). Thomas Coghan, *Haven of Health* (1586), chapters 203, 242. Shakespeare, *Winter's Tale*, Act 4, Scene 3. William Watson, *A Decacordon of Ten Quodlibeticall Questions* (1602), pp. 60, 62, 105, 149. Samuel Hieron, *Works* (ed. 1624), Vol. 1, pp. 9, 88. James Hayward, *Banish'd Virgin* (1635), pp. 114, 140. Matthew Lawrence, *Use and Practice of Faith* (1657), pp. 22, 106, 130, 131. Barrow, *Works* (ed. 1683), Vol. 2, pp. 65, 134, 377. Steele, *Spectator*, Nos. 4, 394, 450.

[4] *Adventurer*, No. 39.

of frequent occurrence in the pages of Coleridge and his imitators.

According to Landor, if we wish to speak of one out of several *means*, we may not, in propriety, even resort to a periphrasis; [1] we must express a plurality, though we intend only a unity. In preference to what is assumed to be bad grammar, on the one hand, and in preference to an affectation, on the other hand, we are counselled to elect a misrepresentation of our meaning. That "this *mean*" is an affectation, just as "this *remain*" would be, is admitted; but that "*this* means" is ungrammatical, postulates a criterion of grammaticalness other than the sole rational criterion, general consent.[2]

---

[1] Gray,—see his *Works* (ed. Mitford, 1858), Vol. 5, p. 208,—commenting, in 1760, on Walpole's *Lives of the Painters*, has the following criticism: "*Geniuses*. There is no such word; and *genii* means something else." Here we are denied a plural. Gray's contemporaries were not, however, so finical as himself, and used *geniuses* freely. I name a few of them. Tilson, Cambridge, J. G. Cooper, and Anon., *World*, Nos. 67, 119, 159, 152, 171. Colman and Thornton, *Connoisseur*, Nos. 19, 28, 47, 54, 70, 72, 139. Richardson, *Correspondence*, Vol. 4, p. 138. Sterne, *Tristram Shandy*, Vol. 2, ch. 19; *Sermons*, No. 42. Miss Carter, *Letters to Miss Talbot*, &c., Vol. 3, p. 165. Jones, of Nayland, *Theological and Miscellaneous Works*, Vol. 5, p. 403. Even Glanvill, in the *Address to the Royal Society*, prefixed to his *Scepsis Scientifica* (ed. 1665), has *geniuses;* and in his *Sadducismus Triumphatus* (ed. 1726), p. 451. And so has Addison, in his remarks on Pavia, Milan, &c., in his *Travels*. In his *Dialogues on Medals*, however, he uses *genies*.

[2] Perhaps "*a* means" sprang from an old oblique case, if it did not originate with the vulgar: compare their *ways*, in "*a* great *ways* off". And so, it may be, we came by our singular *pains*, as in "much *pains is* necessary".

But the singular *means* has other parallels.

Amends. Bp. Pecock, *Repressor*, (1456), p. 110. Barrow, *Works*, Vol. 2, p. 41. Addison, *Spectator*, No. 530. Hughes, *Spectator*, No. 311. Southey, *Life and Correspondence*, Vol. 5, p. 86. I might add references to Lyly, Gabriell Harvey, Hobbes, Milton, Jeremy Collier, and Burke.

Assizes. Henry More, *Mystery of Godliness* (ed. 1660), p. 225. Addison, *Guardian*, No. 105. De Foe's *Political History of the Devil* (ed. 1840), p. 222 (in a quotation). Charles Johnson, *Chrysal* (ed. 1777), Vol. 2, p. 90. Lord Macaulay, *Essay on Warren Hastings*.

Mews, now a singular, was, originally, a plural; and modern usage sanctions, to some extent, the plural *mewses*.

News, to be compared with the French *nouvelles*, has long been, optionally, a singular.

Stews is singular in Raphe Robynson's translation of Sir Thomas More's *Utopia* (1551), p. 43 (ed. 1869); in Gosson's *Schoole of Abuse* (1579), pp. 66, 68 (ed. 1868); and in Lyly's *Euphues* (1579-80), p. 43 (ed. 1868).

Add *odds*, with *ethics, politics, physics, mathematics, mechanics*, and many other names of sciences, now singular.

Alms, bellows, jakes, and *summons* owe their plural aspect to mere corruption; and such is the case with *riches*, which once was of either number. A

Yet it is Landor who lays down, that "one rash decision ruins the judge's credit, which twenty correcter never can restore."

"The epithet 'church-going', applied to a bell, and that by so chaste a writer as Cowper, is an instance of the strange abuses which poets have introduced into their language, till they and their readers take them as matters of course, if they do not single them out expressly as objects of admiration."

It is the poet Wordsworth[1] that thoughtlessly comments thus, by the term "epithet" begging the whole question. Instead of "church-going bell", Cowper ought to have written "churchgoing-bell". "Churchgoing" is here a substantive; and the expression arraigned as an "abuse" stands on the same footing with the elliptical "drinking-cup", "laughing-gas", "riding-whip", "stumbling-block",[2] "walking-stick", "watering-pot", "wedding-garment".

---

like corruption is seen in *gallows*, for which Capgrave has *galow;* while Henry Earl of Monmouth, in his *Advertisements from Parnassus* (1656), has the plural *gallowses* repeatedly. So, too, has John Taylor, the water-poet, at an earlier date. *Shambles* is, as in Shakespeare, singular in Lord Macaulay: see his *Essay on Sir James Mackintosh*. Nash, in his *Christ's Tears over Jerusalem*, has *shamble*. *Tidings* is singular in Gosson's *Schoole of Abuse*, p. 47; *thanks*, in John Taylor's *Works* (ed. 1630), Vol. 2, p. 170, and in Dr. Donne's *Polydoron* (1631), p. 171. "*An* ephemerides." Burton and Fuller. Addison, in the first of his *Dialogues on Medals*, has "*a* tattered *colours*."

Wage might, also, here be remarked on, with the old *victual*, and the comparatively modern *material* and *orgy*. The last is as old as Addison: see the *Spectator*, No. 217. "One *armes*", meaning 'weapon', is found in *Pasquine in a Traunce*, fol. 84; and "an *armes*", in Henry Lawrence's *Of our Communion and Warre with Angels* (1646), p. 172.

Corps, for 'body', whether in its primary sense or in its derivative, was long used as a plural, simply because of its ending in *s*. "All the *corps* of Chrystendome . . . *have* lyved." Sir Thomas More, *Apologye* (1533), fol. 70. Also see Bp. Pearson, *An Exposition of the Creed* (1659), p. 572 (ed. 1845). *Corps* is still the form there found, but for 'dead body.' John Taylor, a generation before, has *corpse*, in the same sense, and as a plural. *Works*, Vol. 2, p. 299. And so has Fuller.

In the last century, if not a little sooner, arose the vulgar *chay*, from the notion that *chaise* was a plural. Then, too, likewise judging by the ear, the uneducated considered *pulse* as a plural, and said "his pulse *are* weak". The singular, if used, must have been, to them, *pul*.

Kickshaws, a barbarization of *quelque chose*, and a plural in virtue of its sound to vulgar ears, has acquired a singular number.

[1] *Poetical Works* (ed. 1846), Vol. 2, p. 342.

[2] Mr. Marsh—*Lectures on the English Language*, p. 656, foot-note,—writes, not very wisely: "Query for the purists: Ought I rather to say, a 'block-that-is-being-stumbled-at?" He fails to see that the first factor of 'stumbling-block' is static, and, consequently, is no longer a participle.

Referring to the word *atonement*, as being explainable by 'a being at one', Coleridge annotates:

"This is a mistaken etymology, and, consequently, a dull, though unintentional, pun. Our *atone* is, doubtless, of the same stock with the Teutonic *aussöhnen, versöhnen;* the Anglo-Saxon taking the *t* for the *s*." [1]

From the air of confidence with which this is said, one would think there must be good foundation for it. On the contrary, it is utterly untenable. *At one*, for 'reconciled', is as old as Roberd Mannyng: "make an *onement* with God", "set *at onement*" [2], are expressions of the sixteenth century; and I am not aware that *atonement* and *atone* are of an earlier date.[3] Further, *atonement* seems to have preceded *atone*. The latter nowhere occurs in the Bible.

"I believe you will very rarely find, in any great writer before the Revolution, the possessive case of an inanimate noun used, in prose, instead of the dependent case; as, 'the watch's hand', for 'the hand of the watch'. The possessive, or Saxon genitive, was confined to persons, or, at least, to animated subjects."

Thus Coleridge again.[4] Yet, even in our Bible and Prayer-book, there are such phrases as "day's journey", "stomach's sake", and "wit's end", with "body's", "eye's", "gospel's", "heaven's", "hope's", "love's", "lucre's", "mercy's", "name's", "oath's", "temple's", "thing's", "tooth's", "truth's," "word's", "work's", &c. &c.; and it may be thought sufficient if I adduce like expressions from Sir Thomas Elyot,[5] Bishop Sanderson,[6]

---

1 *Statesman's Manual*, Appendix A, foot-note.

"You may understand, by *insect*," says Coleridge, in his *Table-talk*, "'life in sections'—diffused generally over the parts." Much in like manner, you may understand, with Joe Miller, *woman* to be made up of *wo* and *man*. An *insect* is so called from the *insections*, 'creases', which characterize its physical structure.

2 Burthogge, in his *Causa Dei* (1675), pp. 172-3, uses the word *atonable*, which is not in the dictionaries. "He, ... by his obedience and death, hath rendred God *attonable* to man."

3 See *The Bible Word-Book*, pp. 42-44. That *one* was anciently pronounced with the vowel-sound of *o* is evident from *only*—formerly written *onely*—and *alone*. The latter word is even found for *all one*, 'all the same'. "It is *alone* as if the Apostle had said," &c. Hieron, *Works*, Vol. 1, p. 525.

4 *Notes and Lectures upon Shakespeare*, &c., Vol. 2, p. 181.

5 "Fortune's mutability", "bed's head". *The Governour*, fol. 95, 157.

6 "Life's", "town's", "merit's." *Sermons* (ed. 1681), Vol. 2, pp. 104, 184, 222.

Hobbes,[1] and Henry More.[2] As to awkward instances of such inflected forms as Coleridge thinks to be modern, I am convinced that they were much more common before the Revolution of 1688 than they have been since.[3]

"The author asks credit for his having, here and elsewhere, resisted the temptation of substituting *whose* for *of which*. The misuse of the said pronoun relative *whose*, where the antecedent neither is, nor is meant to be represented as, personal, or even animal, he would brand as one among the worst of those mimicries of poetic diction by which imbecile writers fancy they elevate their prose,—would, but that, to his vexation, he meets with it, of late, in the compositions of men that least of all need such artifices, and who ought to watch over the purity and privileges of their mother-tongue with all the jealousy of high-priests set apart, by nature, for the pontificate. Poor as our language is in terminations and inflections significant of the genders, to destroy the few it possesses is most wrongful."

Coleridge, here cited once again,[4] implies that he is deal-

---

[1] "Self-defence's", "contract's", "society's", "honour's", "city's". *Works* (ed. Sir W. Molesworth), Vol. 2, pp. 109, 110, 118, 223, 266.

[2] "Sun's", "moon's", "hypocrisy's", "soul's." *Mystery of Godliness*, pp. 344, 345, 385, 440.

[3] Without interruption, we have had, from the days of Anglo-Saxon till the present time, such genitives as Coleridge objects to. Bp. Pecock, in his *Repressor*, pp. 31, 46, 48, &c., prefers "reason's doom" to "doom of reason". "Feet's measures", "summer's day," "the Chirchis bileevyng." *Ibid.*, pp. 25, 89, 137.

We have been altogether capricious with respect to inserting the *s* of the genitive into compounds. Words like *beadsman*, *copesmate*, *cowslip*, *daisy*, and *daysman* are comparatively rare in Old English, while such as *herdman* are very numerous. Thomas Fuller, in his *Mixt Contemplations*, &c. (1660), 2, 2, ventured *seedstime;* but we cling to *seedtime*, though we say *seedsman*. Even *gownsman* and *swordsman* are modernish; *bridemaid* has only lately given place to *bridesmaid;* and *lifeguardmen* was used in 1756: *Connoisseur*, No. 118. *Cow-milk* and *hen-egg* were forms current in the sixteenth century, and perhaps afterwards. The latter of them was not too antique for Dr. Johnson, in his *Journey to the Western Islands of Scotland.*

The genitive case is found in *needs*, *now-a-days*, *always*, *sometimes*, &c. &c. Our *once*, of old written *ones*, is the genitive of *one*. Instead of 'for the *nonce*', we formerly wrote 'for the *nones*', in which *the nones* is a corruption of *then ones;* *then* being the old dative of *the*. A like instance of the provection of *n* is seen in the "*no nother* cause of varyaunce" of Sir Thomas More: *Apologye*, fol. 110. *Nown*, for *own*, occurs in Udal and in Otway; and Shakespeare, John Taylor, and Foote show that *uncle* was long depraved into *nuncle*.

[4] *Notes and Lectures upon Shakespeare*, &c., Vol. 2, p. 354.

Dr. Johnson, in his *Grammar*, states that "*Whose* is rather the poetical than regular genitive of *which*." Bp. Lowth says: "*Whose* is, by some authors, made the possessive case of *which*, and applied to things as well as

ing with a mode of expression which has only recently been authorized by good writers. Nevertheless, the use of *whose* for *of which,* where the antecedent is not only irrational but inanimate, has had the support of high authorities for several hundred years.[1]

persons,—I think, improperly." He then quotes Addison as writing: "Is there any other *doctrine whose* followers are punished?"

According to Mr. Marsh, in language which needs qualifying, "*Whose* was universally employed, as a neuter, by the best English writers, until a recent period, as, in certain combinations, it still is by very good authorities." *Lectures on the English Language*, p. 396. And here I am anxious to confess that I have elsewhere mistaken and misquoted what Mr. Marsh there remarks about the expression "I passed a house *whose* windows were open." If, however, "we should scruple to say" so, my argument is still unaffected.

Our *who* and *what* came from the Anglo-Saxon *hwa* and *hwæt,* which were only interrogative. Of both *hwa* and *hwæt* the genitive was *hwæs,* whence our *whose,* which, as a relative, is older than the relative *who. What,* as strictly equivalent to the relative *which,* never had much vogue, and has long been a vulgarism; but its genitive has survived, in preference to *whichs,* as we should have modernized the medieval *quhilkes.*

Dean Alford, in *The Queen's English,* after asserting, much too roundly, that "both *who* and *which* are, in our older writers, used of persons," asserts, that our ancestors, by their "Our Father *which* art in heaven," intended "reference to the relationship, rather than to the Person only;" for "*who* merely identifies, whereas *which* classifies." The fact is, that the translators of our Bible copied, as far as was practicable, the language of the versions which served as the groundwork of their labours; and that, in 1611, *who,* for *which* as a relative personal pronoun, was not yet thoroughly established. The distinction which the Dean takes is purely gratuitous.

[1] "Langagis *whos* reulis ben not writen." Bp. Pecock, *Repressor,* Introduction, p. lxxxiv., foot-note. Also see pp. 10, 12, 32, 34, 40, 41, &c.

"He mad many bokis of this craft, *whos* names be these," &c. Capgrave, *Chronicle of England,* p. 66.

But I must curtail my references. In those which follow, the words italicized have *whose* for their relative. *Rome, court.* Sir Thomas Elyot, *The Governour,* fol. 196, 197. *Vinegar.* Thomas Coghan, *Haven of Health,* ch. 200. *Antiquity.* Gabriell Harvey, *Pierce's Supererogation* (1593), p. 184 (in *Archaica,* Vol. 2). *Things.* Hobbes, *Works,* Vol. 7, p. 220. *Church.* Henry More, *Mystery of Iniquity* (ed. 1664), p. 541. *America, optics.* Joseph Glanvill, *Scepsis Scientifica,* p. 132; *Plus Ultra* (1668), p. 46. *Things.* Bp. Sanderson, *Sermons,* Vol. 2, p. 152. *Anything.* Cambridge, *The World,* No. 102. *Age, function, wealth, performances.* Charles Johnson, *Chrysal,* Vol. 1, pp. 107, 196; Vol. 2, p. 154; Vol. 3, p. 204. *Trees.* Gray, *Works,* Vol. 4, p. 55. *Field.* Miss Carter, *Letters to Mrs. Montagu,* Vol. 3, p. 22. *Gospel.* William Cowper, *Works* (ed. Southey, 1835—1837), Vol. 4, p. 310. *Bridge.* Southey, *Espriella's Letters,* Vol. 2, p. 267: also see *Letters,* &c. (1797), pp. 34, 62, 92. *Religion, melancholy, perception, columns, buildings, smoke, mountains, fruit, staircase, laurustinus, flowers, arches, power, pedestal, trees.* Shelley, *Essays,* &c., Vol. 1, pp. 34, 234, 242; Vol. 2, pp. 186, 189, 195, 197, 198, 201, 208, 268, 278. "*Work-shop.*" Dr. Arnold, *Life and Correspondence* (ed. 1846), p. 281. *Branch.* Mr. Ruskin, *The Seven Lamps of Architecture,* p. 4: and see pp. iv., 16, 17, 20, 34, 70, 99, 155, 157, 171, 197.

"The word *apartment*, meaning, in effect, a *com*partment of a house, already includes, in its proper sense, a suite of rooms; and it is a mere vulgar error, arising out of the ambitious usage of lodging-house keepers, to talk of one family or one establishment occupying *apartments*, in the plural. 'The queen's *apartment*' at St. James's, or at Versailles, not 'the queen's *apartments*', is the correct expression."

Thus dogmatizes that most wayward of triflers, Mr. Thomas De Quincey,[1] delivering himself in his peculiar manner, as if his own conviction of what is right were conclusive of the ignorance, snobbishness, idiocy, or some other equally deplorable defect, of all dissentients, that is to say, generally, of the world at large. And again:

"Our English use of the word *apartment* is absurd, since it leads to total misconceptions. We read, in French memoirs innumerable, of 'the king's *apartment*', of 'the queen's *apartment*', &c.; and, for us English, the question arises, How? had the king, had her Majesty, only one *room?* But, my friend, they might have a thousand *rooms*, and yet have only one *apartment*. An *apartment* means, in the continental use, a section or *compartment* of an edifice."[2]

Nevertheless, Mr. De Quincey himself stoops, again and again, to "the ambitious usage of lodging-house keepers", and falls into the "mere vulgar error" of using the plural *apartments* for 'rooms'.[3]

The French *appartement* seems to have meant, originally, as it still continues often to mean, 'a storey[4] of a dwelling-house or the like', and thence acquired the signification of 'a suite of rooms'; these being restricted, ordinarily, to one floor: and so our ancestors once understood the word. Viewed etymologically, a *compartment* is one of several parts making up a whole, and may, therefore, be used to

Sir Thomas Elyot has even "diseases . . . against *whom*." *The Governour*, fol. 150. And Shakespeare makes *whom* the relative of *elements*. *Tempest*, Act 3, Scene 2. "Eyelids *who*" and suchlike phrases are common in Shakespeare. Dr. Johnson refers *whom* to a *fowl*, and *who* to an *insect*. *Rasselas*, ch. 1; *Rambler*, No. 93.

[1] *Works* (ed. 1863), Vol. 2, p. 238, foot-note.

[2] *Ibid.*, Vol. 14, p. 458, foot-note.

[3] *Ibid.*, Vol. 10, p. 11; Vol. 11, pp. 62, 66; Vol. 13, p. 241. In *Klosterheim* (ed. 1832), p. 28, the "absurd" use of the singular *apartment*, for 'room', also has the authority of Mr. De Quincey.

[4] It is so defined in Miege's *Great French Dictionary*, 1687-8. M. Littré calls this sense vicious.

describe any room belonging to a set, just as well as any set of rooms among those which compose a house. That which is by itself is *à part*, or 'apart'; and, hence, *apartments* and *compartments* differ, in suggesting aggregates under the aspects, as concerns their constituents, of disjunction and conjunction, respectively. But, as the rooms of a suite, no less than a suite itself, may be regarded singly, our modern use of *apartment* has nothing "absurd" in it. That it arose as Mr. De Quincey asserts is very questionable; it being much more likely that it descended to lodging-house keepers than that it ascended from them. As to its being "a mere vulgar error", or "absurd", who but Mr. De Quincey so esteems it? His "correct expression" is, probably, one of which he enjoys almost the monopoly; unless unidiomatic translators from the French share it with him. His adjudication is, here, irrespective of usage, and, by implication, sets up a standard which none but an autocrat is likely to acknowledge.

And then, what though the French idea of an *apartment* differs from our own? If people who only smatter French fancy themselves masters of it, and fall into "total misconceptions", shall we Gallicize our language, just to prevent such a calamity? Why should "the continental use" of a word be our use, the word having become English? *Apartment* is no longer *appartement*, even as *alter* is not *altérer*. Finally, if *apartment*, for 'room', be "absurd", *funeral*, for our ancient *funerals*, from the still existent *funerailles*, is no entire word, but only a verbal clipping.

Of *civilian* Mr. De Quincey says:[1]

---

[1] *Works*, Vol. 6, p. 79, foot-note. In Vol. 5, p. 138, foot-note, we are told of "the ridiculous abuse of this word *civilian*, in our days."

"Nobody in the world," says Mr. De Quincey, . . . "has less sympathy than myself with idle cavillers, or less indulgence towards the scruples which grow out of excessive puritanism in style." Vol. 5, p. 190. We may believe him; only he disliked, in others, that which was the express image of one of his own most marked peculiarities. He must have reckoned on great inattention, or ignorance, or servility, on the part of his readers, or on all three together.

In the spirit which led him to run amuck at *civilian*, he would have reclaimed *errant*, for *arrant*, and thus made it do double duty. His "*errant* charlatan and impostor,"—Vol. 5, p. 104, in the edition of 1863, and in two other English editions,—as he ought to have seen, is, to common apprehension, almost a tautology; for a charlatan and impostor could scarcely but *err*. When *errant*, as qualifying 'rogue', came to differ from *wandering*, the substitution of the spelling *arrant* was no worse than the change which the word

"Under the fashionable and most childish use of this word, now current,—viz., to indicate simply a non-military person,—a use which has disturbed and perplexed all our past literature for six centuries, it becomes necessary to explain, that, by *civilian* is meant, in English: 1. one who professes and practises the *civil law*, as opposed to the *common* or municipal law of England; 2. one who teaches or expounds this civil law; 3. one who studies it."

Mr. De Quincey, by the way, of course means, his preposterous assertion being interpreted, that the intelligibility of our past literature has been disturbed and perplexed by the emergence and predominance of the use which he stigmatizes as "fashionable and most childish". Not only, however, is this use "fashionable", but its prevalence is well nigh universal. Nor, from their presumptive infrequency, are the chances worth taking into account of the danger of any confusion, in common discourse, between the new sense of the word and its old senses. Why, then, hesitate to accede to so convenient a neoterism? As we needed, in *soldier*, a substantive of *military*, so we needed a substantive of *civil*, as contrasted with *military*. It was aversion to an awkward circumlocution that gave us our modern *civilian*; and no sane argument can invalidate it. Wholly futile, in Mr. De Quincey, otherwise than as throwing light on his unique idiosyncrasy, is his terming it "childish". Such, indeed, or worse, is his perpetual ambition to rehearse the attitude of Athanasius contra mundum.

In his paper on *Anecdotage*, he comments as follows:[1]

"One thing, at least, Miss Hawkins might have learned from Dr. Johnson; and let her not suppose that we say it in ill-nature: she might have learned to weed her pages of many barbarisms in language which now disfigure them; for instance, the barbarism of 'compensate *for* the trouble',—in the very sentence before us,—instead of 'compensate the trouble'."

Here, again, we meet with that arrogant precipitancy without which Mr. De Quincey would lose half his iden-

---

had undergone in meaning. Many of our old expressions have a history corresponding with that of *errant*, 'thorough-paced'. To reanimate this form is impossible, and, if it were possible, would be inexpedient.

[1] *Works*, Vol. 12, pp. 100, 101.

tity.[1] With perfect justice, he elsewhere observes,[2] that, "universally, the class of purists in matters of language are liable to grievous suspicion, as almost constantly proceeding on half-knowledge and on insufficient principles." Dr. Johnson himself[3] has, by a "barbarism", more than once used *compensate* as a neuter verb; and so, doubtless, have scores of reputable writers[4] during the last hundred

---

[1] Intuition stood Mr. De Quincey in poor stead, as an alternative to investigation. Thus, he avers—Vol. 6, p. 157, foot-note,—that, "with the exception of an allusion to the technical usages of horse-racing, and one other, I do not remember that any specific anachronisms, either as to words or things, have been yet pointed out in Chatterton." He could not, then, it seems, even have known, or else he had strangely forgotten, that the spuriousness of Rowley's poems, as productions of the fifteenth century, had been ascertained, past all refuting, by their anachronous *its*.

[2] *Works*, Vol. 14, p. 201, foot-note.

[3] See the *Rambler*, No. 143; *Adventurer*, No. 62.

[4] *Spectator*, No. 581. Miss Carter, *Letters to Miss Talbot*, &c., Vol. 1, p. 122. Hawkesworth, *Adventurer*, No. 1. Dr. Joseph Warton, *Adventurer*, No. 93. Colman, *Adventurer*, No. 90; *English Merchant*, Act 4, Scene 2. Colman and Thornton, *Connoisseur*, Nos. 8, 26. Richardson, *Sir Charles Grandison* (ed. 1811), Vol. 2, p. 143. Bishop Lowth, *Life of William of Wykeham* (ed. 1759), p. 322. Charles Johnson, *Chrysal* (ed. 1777), Vol. 2, p. 7; Vol. 3, pp. 22, 87, 239, 273. Miss Burney, *Evelina* (ed. 1779), Vol. 3, p. 258. Cumberland, *West Indian*, Act 1, Scene 2. *Letters of Junius*, Nos. 11, 36, 38. Burke, *On the Sublime and Beautiful*, Part 2, Section 10; Part 5, Section 6; and often throughout his writings. Sterne, *Letters*, No. 91. Gibbon, *Miscellaneous Works* (ed. 1814), Vol. 3, p. 442; Vol. 4, p. 332. John Frere, *Microcosm*, No. 9. Jones, of Nayland, *Theological and Miscellaneous Works*, Vol. 2, pp. vi., 170; Vol. 6, p. 330. Cowper, *Works*, Vol. 3, pp. 243, 270; Vol. 9, p. 180. Paley, eight times in his *Moral Philosophy*. Godwin, *An Enquiry*, &c. (ed. 1793), p. 679. Miss Carter, *Letters to Mrs. Montagu*, Vol. 2. p. 132; Vol. 3, p. 316. Charles Lamb, *Rosamund Gray*, Chapter 11. Coleridge, *Essays on His Own Times*, pp. 186, 671, 894, 917; *Notes and Lectures upon Shakespeare*, Vol. 1, p. 63; *Church and State*, &c. (ed. 1839), p. 406. Southey, *Life of Wesley* (ed. 1864), Vol. 1, p. 264; *Colloquies*, &c. (ed. 1831), Vol. 1, pp. 209, 273; Vol. 2, pp. 161, 315; *Quarterly Review*; &c. &c. Wordsworth, *Poetical Works*, Vol. 5, p. 357. Dr. Arnold, *Life and Correspondence*, p. 27; *Miscellaneous Works*, pp. 25, 63. Landor, *Works*, Vol. 1, p. 31: *Last Fruit off an Old Tree*, pp. 150, 301. Dr. J. H. Newman, *Essay on the Miracles*, &c., p. 214: *Office and Work of Universities*, p. 66: *Lectures and Essays on University Subjects*, p. 172: *Essays Critical and Historical*, Vol. 1, p. 9; Vol. 2, pp. 87, 384. Bp. Wilberforce, *Addresses*, &c., p. 22. And I might add references to Henry Brooke, Crabbe, Charles Lloyd, Shelley, Hartley Coleridge, Mr. J. S. Mill, &c. &c.

The oldest instance I know is in Barrow. "As if the cross were not enough worthy to *compensate for* our unworthiness." *Works*, Vol. 1, p. 480.

Dr. Johnson, in his Dictionary,—and Dr. Richardson, after him,—overpassed *compensate* as a verb neuter. His editor, Archdeacon Todd, supplied the omission, but on the sole authority of the Rev. Thomas Scott. Saintship, however, is not literature. Dr. Latham leaves the Archdeacon's meagreness where he found it.

and ninety years, Lord Macaulay[1] included. In very many cases we may make *compensate* either neuter or active:[2] the option, like that between *has arrived* and *is arrived*, has the warrant of the best usage. Of this fact Mr. De Quincey either was aware or was unaware. If aware of it, he should have left Miss Hawkins alone; if he was unaware of it, the lady's own authority ought to have led him to suspect that there might be scope for choice in the matter. Sic volo sic jubeo is, too often, the substance and the sum total of an opinionist's judicial equipment.

I next quote part of what Mr. De Quincey[3] says about *implicit*:

"This word is now used in a most ignorant way; and, from its misuse, it has come to be a word wholly useless: for it is now never coupled, I think, with any other substantive than these two, 'faith' and 'confidence',[4]—a poor domain indeed to have sunk to from its original wide range of territory. Moreover, when we say '*implicit* faith', or '*implicit* confidence', we do not thereby indicate any specific *kind* of faith and confidence, differing from other faith, or other confidence: but it is a vague rhetorical word which expresses a great *degree* of faith and confidence; a faith that is unquestioning, a confidence that is unlimited; *i. e.*, in fact, a faith that *is* a faith, a confidence that *is* a confidence.[5] Such a use of the word ought to be abandoned to women."

And how did this use originate? The explanation given is, that the phrase '*implicit* faith', in other words, '*faith by proxy*', employed by "learned assailants of popery", while seen, by "ignorant readers", to be "a term of reproach", was misunderstood by them. "These ignorant

[1] Even in the first chapter of his *History* there are two instances of it.

[2] It is observable that 'compensated *by*', of a thing, not 'compensated *for by*', is the received idiom. Compare 'accepted *by*' and 'approved *by*', though *accept* and *approve* are neuter as well as active.

The following is unidiomatic: "One drawback they have at present, which, I hope, *will be* fully *compensated for* in the future." Mrs. Shelley, in *Shelley Memorials*, p. 107.

[3] *Works*, Vol. 16, pp. 485—489.

[4] In books written by contemporaries of Mr. De Quincey, and which he must have been acquainted with, I find *implicit* qualifying 'assent', 'belief', 'credit', 'deference', 'exactness', 'obedience', 'reception', 'submission', &c. &c.

[5] With what reason could Mr. De Quincey contend that faith and confidence do not admit of degrees, and, unless they are perfect, cannot properly be said to exist?

readers caught at the last *result* of the phrase '*implicit* faith' rightly; truly supposing it to imply a resigned and unquestioning faith; but they missed the whole intermediate cause of meaning, by which only the word *implicit* could ever have been entitled to express that result."

The "true meaning" of the term, Mr. De Quincy contends, is "involved and wrapped up". Edmund Burke, he tells us, employed it in this signification.[1] However, "since his day, I know of no writers who have avoided the slang and unmeaning use of the word, excepting Messrs. Coleridge and Wordsworth."[2] Likewise: "I will be bold to affirm, that no man who had ever acquired a scholar's knowledge of the English language has used the word in that lax and unmeaning way." It follows, therefore, that, so far as Mr. De Quincey was informed, only

---

[1] So far as this sense is conveyed by using *implicit* in antithesis to *express* or *direct*, Mr. De Quincey is right in his assertion: only there his assertions as to Burke should have stopped. But who does not use the word in this sense? Burke will be searched in vain for *implicit* used "accurately," as in the passage, quoted in my text, which Mr. De Quincey foists upon Milton. It will be seen, from the subjoined quotations, that Burke's *implicit* and *implicitly* have nothing peculiar in them whatever.

"And, since it has so happened, and that we owe an *implicit* reverence to all the institutions of our ancestors," &c. *A Vindication of Natural Society.*

"To detect every fallacy, and rectify every mistake, would be endless. It will be enough to point out a few of them, in order to show how unsafe it is to place anything like an *implicit* trust in such a writer." *Observations on a Late State of the Nation.*

"To him the whole nation was to yield an immediate and *implicit* submission." *Thoughts on the Cause of the Present Discontents.*

"If he does not yield an *implicit* unreserved obedience to all his commands," &c. *Speech on Mr. Fox's East-India Bill.*

"His confidence in Mr. Fox was such, and so ample, as to be almost *implicit*." *Substance of the Speech on the Army-estimates*, 1790.

"Mandates issued, which the member is bound blindly and *implicitly* to obey." *Speech at the Conclusion of the Poll*, 1774.

"As to the opinion of the people, which, some think, in such cases, is to be *implicitly* obeyed," &c. *Speech at Bristol*, 1780.

"But, had I stood alone to counsel, and that all were determined to be guided by my advice, and to follow it *implicitly*," &c. *A Letter to a Noble Lord*, 1796.

"Their rights have not been expressly or *implicitly* allowed." *Remarks on the Policy of the Allies.*

[2] Whether Coleridge is to be excepted may be doubtful. "I recommend the fact to the especial attention of those, among ourselves, who are disposed to rest contented with an *implicit* faith and passive acquiescence." *Church and State*, &c., p. 204.

two persons, himself excepted, had, during about two generations, known English thoroughly.[1]

It is further asserted, of *implicit*, that Milton "always uses the word accurately", and that he "speaks of Ezekiel 'swallowing his implicit roll of knowledge'; *i. e.*, coming to the knowledge of many truths, not separately and in detail, but by the act of arriving at some one master-truth which involved all the rest." What Milton[2] really speaks of is "that vision of Ezekiel rolling up her sudden book of implicit knowledge, for him that will to take and swallow down at pleasure." Mr. De Quincey gives us a "roll of knowledge" 'wrapping up' something undisclosed, whereas Milton gives us "knowledge" 'wrapped up' in a visible book. Exposition of realities we are all thankful for; but we have a fair right to reclaim, when the subject-matter of a grave effort of interpretation proves to be a dreamy fiction. Proceeding to build on his forged precedent, Mr. De Quincey prescribes, that, "if any man or government were to suppress a book, that man or government might justly be reproached as the *implicit* destroyer of all the wisdom and virtue that might have been the remote products of that book." This may be received, whenever it shall be evidenced that usage has ratified the employment, in the sense of 'including', of a word which began by signifying 'included'.

What is more, Mr. De Quincey calls on us to credit,

---

[1] Though I have taken but small pains to muster Mr. De Quincey's ignoramuses who have not "ever acquired a scholar's knowledge of the English language," I may as well name such as, in addition to those named further on, I have discovered, after a very short search.

Johnson, *Rambler*, Nos. 35, 39, 56, 74, 127, 155, 158, 171, 176, 184; *Life of Savage*, for "*implicit* follower", "*implicit* confidence", and "*implicit* compliance"; *Life of Swift*, for "*implicitly* to be admitted". Cowper, *Works*, Vol. 15, p. 136. Porson, *Letters to Mr. Archdeacon Travis*, p. 102: *Tracts and Miscellaneous Criticisms*, p. 102. Southey, *Espriella's Letters*, Vol. 2, p. 347; Vol. 3, pp. 139, 230: *Life of Wesley* (ed. 1864), Vol. 1, pp. 82, 295; Vol. 2, pp. 63, 215: *Colloquies*, &c., Vol. 1, p. 167; Vol. 2, pp. 2, 25. Landor, *Last Fruit off an Old Tree*, p. 300. Dr. Newman, *Discussions and Arguments on Various Subjects*, p. 342.

"Mr. Montagu's faith is sincere and *implicit*." "Where else do so many human beings *implicitly* obey one ruling mind?" So writes Lord Macaulay, in his *Essays on Bacon and Mr. Gladstone;* and he expresses himself in the same "most ignorant way" in which people have expressed themselves ever since, I suppose, the word *implicit* came into our language.

Also see the extracts under *implicitly*, cited by Dr. Johnson.

[2] Prefatory Address to *The Doctrine and Discipline of Divorce.*

that not only Milton, but "his contemporaries", always use *implicit* "accurately". That which Mr. De Quincey takes to be its original sense, Milton, on the contrary, very rarely gives to it;[1] and, as for what is alleged to be the sole usage of Milton's contemporaries, considering that Mr. De Quincey was the very pink of Tories and Churchmen, we are at liberty to smile, when it turns out that the precious literary legacy of the Blessed Martyr Charles[2] was not duly present to his memory.

---

[1] "Sects may be in a true church, as well as in a false, when men follow the doctrine too much for the teacher's sake, whom they think almost infallible; and this becomes, through infirmity, *implicit* faith; and the name sectary pertains to such a disciple." *Of True Religion, Heresy*, &c.

"Yet most men, ... through unwillingness to take the pains of understanding their religion by their own diligent study, would fain be saved by a deputy. Hence comes *implicit* faith, ever learning and never taught, much hearing and small proficience, till want of fundamental knowledge easily turns to superstition or popery." *Ibid.*

"Besides, of an *implicit* faith which they profess, the conscience also becomes *implicit*, and so, by voluntary servitude to man's law, forfeits her Christian liberty. Who, then, can plead for such a conscience as, being *implicitly* enthralled to man, instead of God, almost becomes no conscience; as the will, not free, becomes no will?" *A Treatise of Civil Power in Ecclesiastical Causes.*

In these passages, *implicit* means 'dependent', 'on trust', 'submissive', 'servile', 'supine'; and that which, of choice, is genuinely so is 'unreserved', entertaining no doubts and asking no questions. Quite possibly, it was the consideration of the double sense of *implicitus*—to be spoken of presently—that operated to give us the acceptation of *implicit* which I am defending.

[2] "But to binde My selfe to a generall and *implicite* consent to what ever they shall desire or propound . . . . were such a latitude of blinde obedience as never was expected from any freeman, nor fit to be required of any man, much lesse of a King, by his owne subjects," &c. *Eikon Basilike*, chapter 11.

"A perfect slavery of the conscience, and an *implicit* faith that their Prophet is infallible, without any examination and doubt." Henry More, *Mystery of Godliness*, p. 272. Also see p. 546.

"For *implicit* faith is a vertue, where orthodoxie is the object." Glanvill, *Scepsis Scientifica*, p. 95.

"One of the first things they did was to deliver their own minds—and to endeavour the same for others—from the prepossessions and prejudices of complexion, education, and *implicit* authority." *Idem, Essays*, &c. (1676), VII., p. 11.

"Hereupon he requires an absolute obedience from all, without allowing any judgment of discerning; instead thereof, commanding an *implicit* faith;" &c. Timothy Puller, *The Moderation of the Church of England*, &c. (1679), p. 92 (ed. 1843).

"This curious dish
Implicit Walton calls the swallow-fish."
Richard Franck, *Northern Memoirs*, p. 293.

Two only of these passages call for special remark. In that from Glanvill's *Essays*, "*implicit* authority" denotes 'authority *at second hand*,' in con-

Even in classical Latin, *implicitus* signifies 'perplexed', 'confused', as well as 'enveloped'; and its twin participle, *implicatus*, signifies 'obscure'. '*Implicit* faith', almost by a Latinism, defines the faith of the uneducated and irreflective,—as some Frenchman has put it, "the faith of a coal-heaver",[1]—which, of necessity, is vague, dim, imperspicuous, indistinct; and *implicit*, in this expression, comes to have the same meaning, if taken as the antithet of *explicit*.[2] But, notoriously, it is just the assents for which men are unable to render a reason, and which they take on trust, that they hold to both most tenaciously and most unwaveringly;[3] and thus we see that the development of signification which *implicit* has undergone may be accounted for on sound metaphysical principles. For the rest, however this signification arose, the learned world and the

---

tradistinction to that of personal experience. Franck's use of *implicit*, for 'credulously confident,' may be compared with that of Milton, where—see the last note—he applies it, in the sense of 'slavish,' to "conscience."

1 "Implicite [*Fides implicita*]. C'est un terme de Théologie. Foi implicite. C'est une foi obscure, confuse, et qui ne peut être dévelopée par celui qui l'a. C'est la foi du charbonnier." Richelet's *Dictionnaire*, &c. (Amsterdam edition of 1732).

Miege, in his *Great French Dictionary*, before translating our *implicit*, defines it by 'obscure'.

"*Implicit* faith is belief or disbelief without evidence." Dr. John Brown, *An Estimate*, &c. (ed. 1758), Vol. 1, p. 56.

"Nay, there is nothing more undoubtedly true than that great numbers of one side concur, in reality, with the notions of those whom they oppose, were they able to explain their *implicit* sentiments, and to tell their own meaning." Addison, *Freeholder*, No. 54.

"If I had the ill nature of such authors as love to puzzle, I also might leave the foregoing enigma to be solved, or, rather, made more *implicit*, in such ways as philosophy might happen to account for;" &c. Henry Brooke, *The Fool of Quality* (ed. 1792), Vol. 1, p. 203.

Implicit here plainly signifies the opposite of *explicit*, clear, or distinct.

2 Mr. De Quincey says, of *implicit*: "The history of the word is this. *Implicit* (from the Latin *implicitus*, 'involved in', 'folded up') was always used, originally, and still is so by scholars, as the direct antithet of *explicit* (from the Latin *explicitus*, 'evolved', 'unfolded')."

This ignores the fact, that the Latin words had more than one signification apiece. *Implicit* has always had, with us, 'by implication', 'illative', 'deductive', for one of its senses, as applied to things; but the sense specified by Mr. De Quincey was never anything but a rare Latinism.

"Since, therefore, upon account of natural consanguinity, of our best inclinations, of common equity, and general advantage, and an *implicite* compact between men"; &c. Barrow, *Works*, Vol. 1, p. 411.

Implicit here means 'implied,' 'constructive.'

3 "Foi *implicite*, confiance absolue dans les paroles, dans l'autorité de quelqu'un." M. Littré, under his second signification of *implicite*.

unlearned have alike accepted it; and nothing can be idler than Mr. De Quincey's applying to it such designations as "lax", "unmeaning", and "slang".

"Telum imbelle sine ictu
Conjecit."

But let it be admitted that *implicit* reached the sense now generally assigned to it, in the way asserted by Mr. De Quincey; would he repudiate *lot,* for 'collection'? *Lot* first denoted 'portion', and then 'fate';[1] still, though we may "miss the whole intermediate cause of meaning" that led to its being used for 'collection', we are not to be blamed for employing it in that acceptation. A thousand other like instances might easily be adduced. The works of Mr. De Quincey are as full of them as the works of other people; and, if one were to deal by our language at large as he has dealt by *implicit,* there is not a page of his writings but would call for wholesale expurgation.

"Make no mistake, reader," he enjoins,[2] with emphasis

---

[1] *Sort* came into our language with some of its significations already deflected from those of the Latin *sors,* as 'kind', 'manner', &c. It is comparable with *lot,* in that one of its derivative senses has been 'collection'. "Ye shall be slain, all the *sort* of you." *Psalms,* 62, 3, Prayer-book Version. Its primary sense has never been common with us; but Shakespeare has sanctioned it. And so has Robert Southwell. "I intended this comfort to him whom a lamenting *sort* hath left most comfortless." *The Triumphs over Death* (1596), p. viii. (in *Archaica,* Vol. 1).

[2] *Works,* Vol. 6, p. 31, foot-note. Less incautious accounts of the Scriptural meaning of *prophet* occur in Vol. 1, p. 278, foot-note; and in Vol. 16, p. 97, foot-note.

Mr. De Quincey, as his readers will not require to be told, esteemed himself a great theologian and biblicist. In this character, he instructs us, in Vol. 7, p. 218, that "St. Paul is *continually* referring, in his Epistles, to gifts of prophecy." Nowhere does St. Paul speak of "gifts of prophecy"; the expression "gift of prophecy" occurs but once in all his writings; many good expositors take *prophecy* to mean, there, 'vaticination'; and the words "gift of" are an addition by the translators. The apostle's imagined "gifts of prophecy" are again met with in Vol. 1, p. 84, foot-note; and in Vol. 16, p. 97, foot-note. Also see Vol. 13, p. 204.

From an anecdote related in Vol. 13, p. 111, it comes out that *Noe* had never fallen in Mr. De Quincey's way, in the course of his study of the English New Testament. And what could he have supposed there to be in its original? For he sends us to the Septuagint for Νῶε,—"there as plain as a pikestaff," to copy his own expression of his wonderment. In passing, the corrupt *No* which he heard in Westmoreland may have been a tradition based on the Genevan version of the New Testament, once in extensive currency, which has no form but *Noe.* Or it may have descended from the Romish days of England; *Noe* being the name throughout the Vulgate, and in our older literature. Nor is the Patriarch's name, as a monosyllable, unknown. See

ludicrously misplaced. "You, according to modern slang, understand, probably, by a *prophet*, one who foretels coming events. But this is not the Scriptural sense of the word; nor am I aware that it is *once* used, in such a sense, throughout the entire Bible." Mr. De Quincey's Bible must have been sadly mutilated.[1] Besides this, he himself gives in, and without offering apology, to the "slang" sense of *prophet* and several of its conjugates.[2]

"I had observed him sometimes pointing to myself," writes Mr. De Quincey,[3] "and was perplexed at seeing this gesture followed by gloomy looks, and what French reporters call *sensation*, in these young men." Yet elsewhere[4] he has: "The *sensation* which was produced, throughout Germany, by the works in question, is sufficiently evidenced," &c.[5] That which he deems to be the

---

Dr. R. Morris's edition of *The Story of Genesis and Exodus*, lines 557, 566, 580, &c. The following stanza is from a ballad attributed to Richard Tarlton, printed in 1570:

> "The arke of father *Noy*
> Was had in minde as than,
> When God did clene destroy
> Both woman, childe, and man."

In Vol. 7, p. 89, occur, as a quotation, the words "Thereafter as a man sows shall he reap"; and it is pretty evident that Mr. De Quincey thought they were from the Bible. Nowhere in the Bible does *thereafter* occur, in any sense. We find it twice, however, for 'accordingly', in the Prayer-book: *Psalms*, 90, 11, and 111, 10.

Nor was he incapable of the old and vulgar mistake which multiplies St. John's Apocalypse into "the Revelations". See Vol. 6, p. 121, and Vol. 16, p. 377. Addison, Landor, and Dr. Arnold, in the last century and in the present, have fallen into the same error; and so has Mr. Marsh, in his *Lectures on the English Language*, p. 264.

[1] See Deut., 18, 22; Jer., 28, 9; 2 Sam., 24, 11; St. Matthew, 1, 22, and 2, 17; &c. &c.

[2] *Prophet*. Vol. 9, p. 288. *Prophetic*. Vol. 3, pp. 204, 216; Vol. 14, p. 96. *Prophecy*. Vol. 14, p. 41. *Prophesy*. Vol. 7, p. 144.

[3] *Works*, Vol. 14, p. 149.

[4] *Ibid.*, Vol. 16, p. 392.

[5] With similar inconsistency, Coleridge wrote, Feb. 5, 1800, of "the *sensation* excited in the public mind", and, in October of the same year, sneered at "the cant phrase 'made a great *sensation*'." *Essays on His Own Times*, pp. 367, 1021.

Sensation, in the use of it noticed by Mr. De Quincey, is, therefore, much older than the "French reporters" of whom he takes it to be the property.

Completely anachronistic, too, is Landor, where, in an imaginary conversation, he represents Dr. Johnson as saying: "The new and strange word an *individual* seems rather to signify a *dividual* or *par*ticular." *Works*, Vol. 1, p. 164.

If Landor consulted one of Dr. Johnson's octavo editions of his *Dictionary*, he there found, it is true, *individual* called an adjective only; and, in the

English of "French reporters" was good enough English, in the last century, for Jeremy Bentham,[1] and is good enough, in our century, for Lord Macaulay.[2]

"Instead of saying 'sympathy *with* another', many writers", to the serious offence of Mr. De Quincey,[3] "adopt the monstrous barbarism of 'sympathy *for* another'." This "unscholarlike use of the word *sympathy*" is accounted for, he asserts, by the fact, that, "instead of taking it in its proper sense, as the act of reproducing in our minds the feelings of another, whether for hatred, indignation, love, pity, or approbation, it is made a mere synonym of the word *pity*." Not at all. *Fellow-feeling* is, as nearly as possible, equivalent to *sympathy;* and yet we always put *for* after it, just as we may after *compassion*. Usage, and that alone, is to determine our choice of prepositions; and, in language, usage is perpetually changing. 'Influence *into*', 'contemporary *to*', and 'independent *upon*' once were good English; and such 'synonymous *to*' has been within the last hundred years.[4] 'To sympathize *in* the misfortunes of another' does not appear to us a whit stranger than it appeared in the days of Shenstone;[5] "any sympathy *in* her general principles" was the expression preferred by Coleridge,[6] in 1800; and "sympathies

---

absence of extracts, he had reason to conclude that the author did not recognize the word as a substantive. Nor, in the folio edition, is it marked as such; many substantives similarly circumstanced as to evolution being regarded, by the Doctor, as only adjectives. There, however, Bacon, Dryden, and Pope are quoted as having used the word substantivally. But, even if Landor had not found the substantive *individual* in the folio edition, why should he have thought the lexicographer infallible? And does not his etymological objection, such as it is, bear, as against the substantive *individual*, equally against the adjective, in its sole sense countenanced in modern English? Johnson himself, like Lord Macaulay, was decidedly partial to the substantive *individual*. See the *Rambler*, Nos. 4, 6, 57, 99, 104, 146, 148, 171; and the *Adventurer*, Nos. 39, 45, 67. And there are eight instances of it in his *Taxation no Tyranny* alone.

In Henry Earl of Monmouth's *Romulus and Tarquin*, a small duodecimo published in 1637, the substantive *individual* occurs in pp. 61, 139, 140, 218, 250, 271.

I will add, that, to my amusement, I have been warned against this word, by a learned Englishman, on the ground of its being an Americanism.

[1] *The Church of England Catechism Examined* (ed. 1868), p. 2.

[2] *History of England*, Chapters 14, 22.

[3] *Works*, Vol. 13, p. 195, foot-note.

[4] See Bp. Lowth's *Isaiah* (ed. 1778), Preliminary Dissertation, pp. 38, 39, 40.

[5] See his *Letters*, No. 70.

[6] *Essays on His Own Times*, p. 390.

toward" may claim the sanction of Landor.[1] '*Sympathy for*' has the consentient authority of Sterne,[2] Gray,[3] Burke,[4] Wordsworth,[5] Lord Macaulay,[6] Dr. Newman,[7] and Mr Ruskin;[8] and the world will, in all likelihood, reckon them quite as good judges, in a matter of "monstrous barbarism," as Mr. De Quincey.[9]

In short, our language, as practically exemplified, is in most deplorable case, if we are to abide by his opinion.

> "With the single exception of William Wordsworth, who has paid an honourable attention to the purity and accuracy of his English, we believe that there is not one celebrated author of this day who has written two pages consecutively, without some flagrant impropriety in the grammar,—such as the eternal confusion[10] of the preterite with the past participle, confusion of verbs transitive with intransitive, &c.,—or some violation, more or less, of the vernacular idiom."

We are also apprised that Coleridge and Wordsworth, "but especially the last, have been remarkably attentive to the scholarlike use of words, and to the history of their own language".[11] Most certainly, their English is, in

---

[1] *Last Fruit off an Old Tree*, p. 195. [2] "Sympathy *for* the poor fellow's distress." *Tristram Shandy*, Vol. 2, Ch. 17. "A sort of sympathy *for* your afflictions." *Letters*, No. 120. [3] *Works*, Vol. 5, p. 304.

[4] "In order to awaken something of sympathy *for* the unfortunate natives." *Speech on Mr. Fox's East-India Bill.*

[5] "The man who, in this age, feels no regret for the ruined honour of other nations must be poor in sympathy *for* the honour of his own country." *Concerning the Relations of Great Britain, Spain, and Portugal*, p. 169.

[6] *Essays on Hallam, Lord Bacon, and Warren Hastings.* In two of the passages here referred to, the sympathy is for persons. [7] *Essays Critical and Historical*, Vol. 1, Dedication: *Discussions and Arguments on Various Subjects*, p. 380. [8] *The Seven Lamps of Architecture*, p. 65.

[9] We are not expressly forbidden, by Mr. De Quincey, to have sympathy *for an object*, *in* it, or *towards* it. But he as good as disallows these forms of speech; since, according to him, *sympathy*, as not being followed by *with*, is here misemployed for *pity*. He, however, writes—Vol. 1, p. 40,—of "sympathies *in* the problems suggested by books." The facts escaped him, that we often use *sympathy* in the sense of 'sympathetic interest', and that we then allow ourselves a variety of prepositions after it.

In Robert Southwell's *Triumphs over Death*, p. 2, piety is said to be "a mutual *sympathy*, in each, *of* other's misery." This use is, I believe, very rare.

[10] *Works*, Vol. 10, pp. 71, 72. A more exact writer than Mr. De Quincey would, assuredly, have preferred "*perpetual* confusion." Wordsworth's and Coleridge's *holden*, by the way, he does not seem to have regarded as imitable.

[11] *Works*, Vol. 16, p. 487. "In Spenser, in Shakespeare, in the Bible of King James's reign, and in Milton, there are very few grammatical errors."

many points, highly commendable; and their judgments as to what is allowable in phraseology are blemished by few crotchets. For instance, as we have seen, neither of them shrank from what was, to Mr. De Quincey, a "barbarism", 'compensate *for*'; and the latter could perpetrate "the monstrous barbarism" 'sympathy *for*'. At the same time, it may be gravely doubted whether they would have tolerated Mr. De Quincey's "he again *laid* down, and addressed himself to sleep",[1] "he must have *rode* along with the orchestral charge",[2] "she was long *of* returning to herself",[3] and the equally gross Scotticism of using *that* for *in that, for that,* or *because.*[4] But the reader must have

Vol. 8, p. 15. Elsewhere, one, at least, of these authorities in grammar is decreed to be impeccable. "It makes us blush to add, that even grammar is so little of a perfect attainment amongst us, that, with two or three exceptions,—one being Shakespeare, whom some affect to consider as belonging to a semi-barbarous age,—we have never seen the writer, through a circuit of prodigious reading, who has not sometimes violated the accidence or the syntax of English grammar." Vol. 10, p. 198. The true standard of grammaticalness in English was known, and in its plenitude, to Mr. De Quincey; only the secret was too choice to be imparted to an unappreciative public. But why did he cast even a single pearl before swine?

[1] *Klosterheim*, p. 73. [2] *Works*, Vol. 13, p. 215. [3] *Ibid.*, Vol. 16, p. 297.

[4] *Ibid.*, Vol. 5, p. 160; Vol. 6, p. 235: *Klosterheim*, p. 112. It is no defence of a Scotticism, that once it was English.

Page upon page might be filled with specimens of Mr. De Quincey's bad or dubious English. A few samples are subjoined.

"A *reciprocal* messenger between the prophet and heaven." Vol. 1, p. 47.

"No part, that is to say, but *what* acts on the whole." Vol. 1, p. 255.

"Few people have lived on such terms of entire harmony and affection *as he lived* with the woman of his final choice." Vol. 2, p. 190.

"When next you see the bird which now perches above your head, you will *only have* five days more to live." Vol. 3, p. 319.

"To sketch the history of the art, and to examine its principles critically, now remains as a duty for the connoisseur, and for judges of quite *another* stamp *from* his Majesty's Judges of Assize." Vol. 4, p. 4.

"But the fundus . . . . must for ever be sought in one and the same field, viz., the *ludicrous of* incident, or the *ludicrous of* situation," &c. Vol. 8, p. 54.

"One man might steal a horse with more hope of indulgence *than another could look over the hedge.*" Vol. 9, p. 32.

"It was his intention, as I am well assured, just about the time that he took his flight for Elysium, to *have commenced* regular contributor to your journal." Vol. 11, pp. 114, 115. Also see Vol. 16, p. 338.

"But can any gravity stand the *ridicule* of a father's sitting down to examine his child's features by his own?" Vol. 12, p. 198.

"Even twelve or fifteen years ago, I *have seen* French circulating libraries in London," &c. Vol. 13, p. 40, foot-note.

"And, apart from that objection, at this period, the hasty unfolding of far *different* intellectual interests *than* such as belong to mere literature had," &c. Vol. 14, p. 359.

had enough for once of a man who seldom takes a word in hand to discourse on, without making some ridiculous misstatement. For his knowledge of English, so far as it surpassed that of his most commonplace neighbours, he would well have followed the advice of Dogberry, to "give God thanks, and make no boast of it". The truth appears to be, that he prized the character of being a correct writer, in proportion to the pains which it cost him to support it; and his success in supporting it was not, after all, of the most brilliant. Something vastly better than that which, whether as a verbal critic or as a general essayist, he has bequeathed to us ought, surely, to have been expected from one who laid claim to "the advantage of a prodigious memory, and the far greater advantage of a logical instinct for feeling, in a moment, the secret analogies or parallelisms that connected things else apparently remote", together with "an inexhaustible fertility of topics, and, therefore, of resources for illustrating or for varying any subject that chance or purpose suggested";[1] who complacently ranked himself among "elaborate scholars";[2] who professed to

---

"It is certain that no very great man has ever existed, *but that* his greatness has been rehearsed and predicted in one or other of his parents." Vol. 15, p. 29.

"After all, that is not of a deeper tinge than I have seen *amongst many an Englishman.*" Vol. 16, p. 283.

"Sentence was passed; and the punishment was to be inflicted on two separate days, with *an interval between each,*" &c. Vol. 16, p. 340.

"I have, myself, travelled by coaches *who* were rapidly nearing the point," &c. *Logic of Political Economy*, p. 235.

It may be submitted, with all confidence, whether these blunders are not, mostly, such as any man of decent education would be ashamed to be guilty of even in his most unguarded chitchat. Yet Archbishop Trench, in 1859, pronounced Mr. De Quincey to be the person "whom I must needs esteem the greatest living master of our English tongue." *English, Past and Present* (4th ed.), p. 32.

The authority of Mr. De Quincey, whatever may be my own valuation of it, is of great weight with many. I shall, therefore, appeal to it, wherever it may suit my purpose to do so.

[1] *Works*, Vol. 1, p. 135.

[2] *Ibid.*, Vol. 9, p. 20. It must have been from what Mr. De Quincey happily calls the overmastering habit of stating everything "in a spirit of amplification, with a view to the wonder only of the reader", that he was induced to speak as he has spoken of numerous literary celebrities. "Hazlitt had read nothing"; "Rousseau, like William Wordsworth, had read, at the outside, twelve volumes octavo, in his whole lifetime"; and Porson's "knowledge of English was so limited, that his total cargo might have been embarked on board a walnut-shell, on the bosom of a slop-bason, and insured for three half-pence". Vol. 8, pp. 127, 173, 313. Edmund Burke "was

have travelled through "a circuit of prodigious reading";[1] and who had "been studying English for thirty years and upwards".[2] No one has ever demonstrated more satisfactorily, in his own person, what he was so keenly sensible of, as concerned others, "the danger, in critical niceties, of trusting to any single memory, though the best in the world".[3] Nor, save that his fame is much greater in America than it is in England, should I have utilized him to the end of making manifest the hazard incurred by such as dogmatize rashly,

"And what their narrow science mocks
Damn with the name of heterodox."

The *Athenæum*, a few years ago,[4] published a letter in which the word *curious*, as now most commonly employed, was assailed with great vehemence. The use referred to is that which, we are told, makes the word a synonym of "strange" or "extraordinary"; though I should prefer to say, 'novel', 'unusual', or, more generally, 'novel and noticeable'. "This use of the word", the letter-writer objects, "is at once novel and absurd, and, I cannot but think, unknown in the writings of every good author." Wrought upon by this supposed discovery, at least a dozen different correspondents, writing in journals which fell in my way, rushed into publicity, to assist in its promulgation; and, in some American book[5] which I have not at hand, the *Athenæum* letter was reprinted in full, and without comment. There seems to be no doubt, that, to many minds, almost any statement, if not palpably incredible, is invested with validity by the bare circumstance of being put in black and white.

The truth, I believe, as concerns the sense of *curious* under consideration, is, that, from Queen Anne's time down to the present day, very few authors have not employed it.[6] That, in the mean time, it has escaped the

---

the most double-minded person in the world"; and Lindley Murray, an American, is called "an imbecile stranger." Vol. 10, pp. 54, 71. Dr. Johnson "had studied nothing"; and Boileau and Addison were "neither of them accomplished in scholarship". Vol. 13, pp. 161, 203.

[1] *Works*, Vol. 10, p. 198. Not the circuit, be it observed, of his reading was "prodigious", but the reading itself.

[2] *Works*, Vol. 8, p. 314. [3] *Ibid.*, Vol. 6, p. 160. [4] March 24, 1866.

[5] Mr. Edward S. Gould's *Good English*, if my memory serves me faithfully.

[6] It was not unknown, however, in the sixteenth and seventeenth centuries

indolence of all our lexicographers but the most recent will not seem remarkable to any one conversant with the shortcomings[1] of our lexicographers. To Addison[2] it was

---

"Some of old time put great superstition in characters *curiously* engraved in theyr Pentagonon," &c. Nash, *Pierce Penilesse his Supplication to the Devill* (1592), p. 86 (ed. 1842).

"All [language] must be affected and preposterous, ... it is so *curious.*" Ben Jonson, *Timber, De vere Argutis.*

"It were no lesse rare to observe some of our women who stand most affected to *curious* apparell." R. Brathwait, *A Boulster-lecture* (1640), p. 202.

"For their places of pleasure, they are in their groves, where their *curious* fruit-trees, before described, grow", &c. Edward Terry, *A Voyage to East India*, pp. 200, 201.

Also see the translation of *Il Cardinalismo di Santa Chiesa* (1670), pp. 6, 45, 77, 95, 246.

Incurious, as the opposite of the objective *curious* here contemplated, is not unexampled. "In confirmation of these truths, we may conclude this part of our subject with a not *incurious* anecdote." Dr. John Brown, *An Estimate*, &c., Vol. 1, p. 57. Also see p. 137; and Vol. 2, p. 99. Horace Walpole uses *incurious* in the same way.

Curiosity was long ago used where we now use, more frequently, *curiousness.* "At a convenient distance from them appear'd the Doriphori, ... whom the gorgiousnesse of their habit, and *curiosity* of their arms, rendred almost of no defence." *Cassandra* (ed. 1652), Vol. 1, p. 182.

[1] Writing in 1847, Mr. De Quincey, with his usual bile and bluster, stigmatized this expression as "horridly tabernacular, and such that no gentleman could allow himself to touch it without gloves." *Works*, Vol. 7, p. 89. As we all know, it is, now, of unchallenged respectability.

The clause just transcribed is adduced, by Dr. Webster's editors, to illustrate their third definition of *tabernacular*: "Of, or belonging to, a booth or shop; hence, common; low." A good sample, this, of pure moonshine. It would be interesting to know how the learned divines aforesaid would elucidate Crabbe, where he writes:

"See yonder preacher to his people pass,
Borne up and swelled by *tabernacle-gas.*"

The shed in Moorfields, which Whitefield used as a temporary chapel, was called *The Tabernacle*; and, in the scornful dialect of certain Church-of-Englandmen, Methodist and such-like places of worship have, since then, been known as *tabernacles.* Hence Mr. De Quincey's *tabernacular.*

Southey, that pattern of political piety, more than once, in the *Quarterly Review*, has the synonymous *schism-shop*; and the old Puritans termed churches *steeple-houses.* An established religion is, of necessity, contemptuous towards its depressed rivals; these retaliate the disdain of which they are the objects; and careless Gallios infer that the message which all alike have heard from the beginning must be, that they should hate one another. See 1 John, 3, 11.

[2] "I shall beg leave to explain myself in a matter which is *curious* in its kind, and which none of the critics have treated of." *Spectator*, No. 357. Also see Nos. 83, 267, 391.

"Nothing could be more *curious* than to see those little animals about such a work." *Guardian*, No. 157. Also see No. 156.

good English; and Gray,[1] Johnson,[2] Burke,[3] Cowper,[4] Coleridge,[5] Southey,[6] and Lord Macaulay[7] have agreed with him in so esteeming it. As will be seen, on verifying the references given at the foot of the page, expressions having *it is*, or the like, prefixed to *curious*, which the censurer of the simple adjective finds peculiarly exceptionable, are, likewise, perfectly classical; and so is *curiously*, for 'observably'.[8]

Curious, in its more modern acceptation, is not, then, "novel"; and it is very far indeed from being "unknown in the writings of every good author". And no more is it "absurd". First the word denoted a state of mind, interest or diligence in inquiry or prosecution; then it was predicated of things which exhibit evident tokens of care (*cura*), dexterous application, ingenuity;[9] and, as

---

1 "Your opinion of Diodorus is, doubtless, right; but there are things in him very *curious*, got out of better authorities now lost." *Works*, Vol. 3, p. 53. I have observed fifteen like instances in Gray.

2 "I could command whatever was imported, *curious* or valuable." *Rambler*, No. 181.

"A very *curious* book might be written on the 'Fortune of Physicians'." *Life of Akenside*.

3 "To this purpose Mr. Spon . . . . gives us a *curious* story," &c. *On the Sublime and Beautiful*, Part 4, Sect. 4.

4 "I despair now of making any *curious* discoveries about him." *Works*, Vol. 7, p. 226. Other instances might be added.

5 *Essays on His Own Times*, pp. 363, 380, 399, &c. &c. "A *curious* anomaly." *Church and State*, &c., p. 410.

6 *Letters*, &c. (1797), pp. 10, 15, 109, &c. &c.

7 "That unfortunate book contained much that was *curious* and interesting." *Essay on Madame D'Arblay*.

Additionally, I might refer to Henry Carey, Aaron Hill, Richardson, the Earl of Cork, Miss Carter, Miss Talbot, Miss Burney, Horace Walpole, Colman, Foote, Cumberland, Bentham, Wordsworth, Landor, Dr. Newman, Mr. J. S. Mill, and Mr. Gladstone.

8 *It is curious*, &c. Sir Joshua Reynolds, *Idler*, No. 76. Burke, *Speech on Conciliation with America*, &c. &c. Porson, *Letters to Mr. Archdeacon Travis*, p. 168: *Tracts and Miscellaneous Criticisms*, p. 319. Southey, *Colloquies*, &c., Vol. 2, p. 240. Charles Lamb, *Letters* (ed. 1837), Vol. 1, pp. 184, 268. Landor, *Dry Sticks Fagoted*, p. 124: *Last Fruit off an Old Tree*, pp. 166, 341. Lord Macaulay, *Essays on Lord Mahon, Horace Walpole, Sir William Temple, and Mirabeau: Speeches* (ed. 1854), p. 82. Mr. Ruskin, *The Seven Lamps of Architecture*, pp. 110, 173.

Curiously enough, &c. Southey, *Cowper's Works*, Vol. 3, pp. 84, 212. Lord Macaulay, *Essay on Addison*. Dr. Newman, *Office and Work of Universities*, p. 210.

9 In the "*curious* arts" of Acts, 19, 19, *curious* is objective; but its sense is peculiar. Magic is there indicated; and its practitioners were reckoned not simply inquisitive, but unduly so.

such things are out of the common, and are apt to arrest attention, it naturally acquired the sense which has been thoughtlessly arraigned as contrary to reason.[1] The second signification, 'executed with thought and skill', almost, in fact, denotes the objective correlative of that which is denoted by the first signification. *Nice*,[2] before it meant 'agreeable', meant 'fastidious'; *dreadful* and *frightful* had, of old, the significations 'full of dread' and 'full of fright'; and all languages supply, in the secondary acceptations of words, liberal illustrations of objective developments from subjective originals. If the person who objected to the latest use of *curious* had generalized his objection, and, especially, if he had applied it impartially to our language at large, he would have found himself hampered by consequences which he little expected. Even as to *curious* itself, he would have had to alter not only Shakespeare's "*curious* bed", "most *curious* mantle", and "*curious* tale", but our Bible, with its "*curious* girdle" and "*curious* works". Our familiar *curiosities*, for 'rarities', would, also, in consistency, fall under the ban of this unreflecting denunciator.

Curious, in the *Apocrypha*,—and only there in the whole *Bible*,—signifies 'inquisitive', and nothing else.

[1] Addison writes of "a punch-bowl, painted upon a sign near Charing-cross, and very *curiously* garnished with a couple of angels hovering over it, and squeezing a lemon into it". *Spectator*, No. 28. *Curiously* here means 'in a novel and striking way', quite as well as 'artfully', 'ingeniously'.

Dr. Johnson's eighth definition of *curious* is "elegant, neat, laboured, finished"; and the transition thence to the latest sense of the word—which he has passed over,—might almost have been predicted.

In French, Italian, &c., the words etymologically corresponding to our *curious* have all the three acceptations which I have noted above.

[2] "*Nice* and *dear* are the great To Prepon and To Kalon of feminine conversational moralities." So writes Lord Lytton, in his *England and the English*. To Mr. De Quincey,—*Works*, Vol. 16, p. 487, foot-note,—this use of *nice* ranks "among the most shocking of the unscholarlike barbarisms now prevalent". *Nice*, by his legislation, "does not and *cannot* express a quality of the object, but merely a quality of the subject". But the ladies reject all such straitened views of the limits of possibility; and, as to *nice*, they have proved, with the very general concurrence of their lords, that what is infeasible in theory may easily be realized in practice.

Nor is this use of *nice* a product of our times. The learned Miss Carter wrote, in 1769: "I intend to dine with Mrs. Borgrave, and, in the evening, take a *nice* walk." *Letters to Mrs. Montagu*, Vol. 2, p. 34. "A very *nice* letter." *Ibid.*, Vol. 3, p. 200. And Charles Johnson wrote "sweet-breads and cock's combs . . . are very *nice*", "*nice* bits", "a *nice* leg of a fowl", "*nice* little things". *Chrysal*, Vol. 2, pp. 9, 153; Vol. 3, p. 72; Vol. 4, p. 203.

The Rev. Mr. Blackley, in his *Word Gossip*, has propounded, with all the positiveness befitting accredited inerrancy, a new faith touching the derivation of *parson* and *parishioner*. It is unfortunate, for this gentleman, that philology is not theology, and that his authority is otherwise than autocratic. If, notwithstanding his sacred character, he will deal with matters of this world, it must be on the same conditions, as regards liability to protest, which attach to those whom such matters interest more particularly.

To connect *parson*, etymologically, with *person* he boldly affirms to be a "ridiculous error". Blackstone, who so connected it, "though a good lawyer, was but an indifferent philologer, or he would have observed the necessary connexion between *parson* and *parish*, specially illustrated by the existence of the word *parishioner*"; and he is gratuitously taxed with "implying that the *parson* of a parish was, in theory, what he, certainly, is not, necessarily, in fact, *the person*, the individual, of most importance in a parish". And now for—not to shock a clergyman by profanely applying the term *revelation*,—the new patefaction:

> "The word *parson* is, in fact, equivalent to *parishion*, a compression of *parochianus*, which, as a substantive, means *one belonging to a parish*. We English have taken *parochianus* in one sense, *parson*, for the minister *belonging to a parish*; the French have taken it in another, *paroissien*, the inhabitant *belonging to a parish*; and, when our language needed to describe members of the parson's flock, the form equivalent to *paroissien* being already usurped in *parson*, it was obliged to form the word *parishioner*, as implying the relation of the ordinary resident to the appointed minister in a parish."

On the true origin of *parson*, which has no connexion whatever with *parish*, or with any similar word, there is but little to add to what Dr. John Cowell wrote,[1] more than two centuries ago:

---

[1] In *The Interpreter* (1637). Coleridge thus explains *parson*: "*Persona κατ' ἐξοχήν*; *persona exemplaris*; the representative and exemplar of the personal character of the community or parish; of their duties and rights, of their hopes, privileges, and requisite qualifications, as moral persons, and not merely living things." *Church and State*, &c., p. 156, first foot-note. Coleridge should have given notice that this was only his personal idea of a *parson*.

"*Parson* (*persona*) commeth of the French (*personne*). It peculiarly signifieth, with us, the rector of a church; the reason whereof seèmeth to bee, because hee, for his time, representeth the church, and susteineth the person thereof, as well in siewing as being siewed in any action touching the same."

We are told that *parishion* is compressed from *parochianus;* and it is implied that *parson* is compressed from *parishion*.[1] But why go to Low Latin, rather than to Old French, for the source of *parishion?* And what proof is there that *parishion* ever meant 'parson'? Mr. Blackley here palms upon his readers a word which, to him, was, evidently enough, a mere assumption. Having, though unconfessedly, coined it, he proceeds to coin a sense for it; in the next place, he contracts it, by squeezing out two vowels and a consonant; and, lastly, he is ready to wax uncomplimentary, if you hesitate to accept his conclusion as to how we came by *parson*.

I may add, that this term, in the form *person,* was used, by Myrc,[2] in the twelfth century, down to which time, as has been the case ever since, a *parson* is not known to have been denominated, in English, by any word allied to *parish*.

Forging history, after the manner here exposed, and dispensing the spurious product as a genuine article, would, in a layman, be a somewhat hardy procedure.[3]

Some choice eloquence about priestcraft, with which

---

[1] Skinner long ago broached this untenable view, taking *parson* from "*parishon*, ecclesiastes"; and Dr. Richardson adopts it. Neither of them gives any example of *parishon* used in the sense required to uphold their whim.

As will shortly be seen, *parishon* preceded *parishioner*, and meant the same.

Charles Lamb uses *diocesan*,—as a Frenchman might use *diocésain*,—for 'a person living under the head of a diocese'. See his *Valentine's Day*, in *Elia's Essays*. And once this was allowable English, according to Dr. Richardson's Dictionary.

[2] *Instructions for Parish Priests*, p. 22.

[3] The contents of *Word Gossip* first appeared in a religious magazine for children. At pp. 65, 66, Mr. Blackley, after saying that "we are unwilling to speak of a milliner, or a barmaid, as a young *lady*", adds: "though, indeed, American notions would scout such hesitation". An English clergyman would be an unusually favourable specimen of his class, if he denied himself an opportunity of insinuating contempt for Americans. Whether the truth is told, or not, is quite a secondary consideration. No slander is more sedulously inculcated, in England, than the slander that we Americans aim at breaking down all social distinctions.

Mr. Blackley is inspired by the Blackstonian heresy, need not be quoted. To exalt a clergyman beyond what is due is, in his eyes, highly pernicious. Is it, however, less pernicious to depress a layman beyond what is due, in making a *parishioner*, on the very showing of his appellative, a mere adjunct to his "parishion" or *parson?* The odd facts, by the by, on the new view, first, that our ancestors went back to *parishion* and made *parishioner*, and did not, instead, make *parsoner* from *parson*, and, secondly, that, if *parishioner* was used contemporaneously with *parishion*, the longer word should have come down unabridged, and the shorter should have been abridged, Mr. Blackley sagaciously forbears calling attention to.

To the Old French *parrochia, parroquia, paroche*,—afterwards modified into *paroisse*,—we owe, directly, the early English forms of what we have long written *parish*. In the twelfth century, we had *paresche, paresch*, and *parisse;*[1] in the thirteenth century, *paroche;* and Chaucer writes *parisch*.[2] Similarly, as the Old French had the derivatives *parrochian, paroquian*, we had *paresschen, pareschen*,[3] *paraschen, parachen*,[4] *parishen, parysshen*,[5] *parischen*,[6] *parisschen*,[7] *pareshon*,[8] &c., for 'inhabitant of a parish'. By the addition of *-er* to a corruption of the French word, it is reasonable to suppose, we obtained our *parishioner;*[9] just as we are indebted, for *practitioner*, to the addition of *-er* to a corruption of *praticien*.[10] This ex-

---

1 Myrc's *Instructions*, &c., pp. 1, 7, 22.

2 See Mr. Stratmann's *Dictionary of the Old English Language*, &c. Krefeld: 1867.

3 Myrc's *Instructions*, &c., pp. 25, 26.

4 Pecock's *Repressor*, &c., pp. 391, 393, 416.

5 *Political Poems and Songs*, &c. (edited by Mr. Thomas Wright), Vol. 1, p. 327; Vol. 2, p. 217.

6 *Religious Pieces in Prose and Verse* (edited by the Rev. G. G. Perry), p. 2. Chaucer and Pecock have the same form.

7 Langland, *The Vision of William concerning Piers Plowman* (1362), Text A (ed. Rev. W. A. Skeat), p. 5.

8 *Revelation to the Monk of Evesham*, p. 49. *Paryshons* and *parishons*, at p. 104, seem to stand for *parishes:* but this cannot well be.

9 Bishop Hall uses *parishional*, in the expression "*parishionall* meetings". Strictly, *parishional* ought to mean 'pertaining to *parishioners*', rather than 'pertaining to a *parish*'. It is such a word as our *congressional* is, and such a word as *processional* would be, if used to mean 'pertaining to a *process*'.

10 Coleridge ventured to Anglicize this into *practician;* and Brathwait, in *A Boulster-lecture* (1640), p. 307, uses the substantive *practist*. *Practition*, the base of *practitioner*, though I have nowhere happened on it, very likely

planation of the origin of *parishioner* is, so far as I know, now first suggested.[1]

Among the illaudable characteristics of Professor Maximilian Müller,[2] his facility of assertion is conspicuous. For instance,[3] he lays down that our word *church* came into England through the Latin, and that it was brought by "the Christian missionaries and priests, from the time of St. Augustine's landing, in 597, to the time of Alfred". But affirmantis est probare; and, before all this can be taken as prescribed, a question or two may be allowed to a sceptic. Can it be shown—since we are told "*kyriake* ≐ *church*",—that *kyriake* was ever used in ecclesiastical Latin? Can it even be shown that κυριακή—though it meant 'Sunday',—ever meant 'church'? Who can say that *church*, whatever it was derived from, was not in use, in some old form, before the days of St. Augustine and his successors? And who can say that it may not, after all, be a corruption of ἐκκλησία?[4] Philology becomes an easy affair enough, when, from premises to conclusion, it takes the shape of an exercise of the imagination; and "the science of language", as thus illustrated by its chief hierophant, reveals itself as indeed a science of a brand-new description.

If I decline to descant on critics such as Dean Alford and

---

was once used. We have had, somewhat akin to *parishional*, *practitional*. "Ambitious *practitionall* state Jesuits." W. Watson, *A Decacordon*, &c., p. 201. And it has been used in modern times. See *Selections from the Letters of Robert Southey*, Vol. 2, p. 1.

Magition, *musition*, and *phisition*, for *magician*, &c., were common spellings in the sixteenth century, and on into the seventeenth.

Both *parishioner* and *practitioner* occur in Latimer, as quoted by Dr. Richardson. These forms, in an age when our language was scarcely thought to come within the purview of philology, may have recommended themselves, as offering to the eye derivatives of the type of *executioner*, *extortioner*, &c.

[1] *Fruiterer* is a corruption of the French *fruitier;* and *fripperer*, shortened to *fripper*, of the French *frippier:* but, in *poulterer*, there is a double ending; the old word being *poulter*. So, *upholsterer* has been elongated from *upholster*. *Lesserer* is still used, in some parts of England, for *lesser* or *less*. *Fischerer*, for *fisher*, occurs in Capgrave's *Chronicle*, p. 113. *Musicianer* is not yet obsolete. The modern *chickens* contains an *s* added to *chicken*, itself a plural.

[2] That he can borrow freely, without recognizable acknowledgment, is shown in the *Transactions of the Philological Society*, 1862-3, p. 117, footnote.

[3] *Lectures on the Science of Language*, Vol. 2, pp. 268, 269.

[4] More than twenty years ago, I elaborated an argument for this etymology; and I still think it much more likely that *church* came from ἐκκλησία than from any derivative of κύριος.

Mr. Moon, it is not because of any poverty of matter for remark in the headlong sciolism of the one and in the piddling pedagoguery of the other. But hasty and shallow philologizing is everywhere common, and no less so in America than in England. Partly to keep Mr. Richard Grant White in countenance, and partly because, on cursorily turning over the leaves of his *Words and Their Uses,* I was reminded of certain old-world specimens of precipitate speculation, I have been at the trouble of this long preliminary. The special reminders of those specimens shall now be considered; and, if they are made the subject of some detail, it is with design to show irrefutably, among divers ends, what is likely, in our day, to happen to one who puts his faith over-confidingly in dictionaries and intuition.

The verb *experience* is, to Mr. White, parroting Dean Alford,[1] altogether objectionable. It is, further, significant, that he thinks it to be of rare occurrence in good writers. "I have been able to find, by diligent search, only one example of any authority", he informs us; and that example, taken from the *Guardian,* he discovers in Dr. Richardson's Dictionary. Since "diligent search" may mean, with Mr. White, industry in turning over the pages of dictionaries, one can scarcely wonder at the generality of his conclusions.[2] Dr. Johnson observes, in the Preface to his Dictionary: "It is remarkable, that, in reviewing my collection, I found the word *sea* unexemplified." No less remarkable is it, that he has treated the verb *experience* inadequately,[3] considering his liking for

[1] "Some years ago, precise scholars used to exclaim against the verb *to experience;* and a very ugly candidate for admission into the language it was. . . . No instance of the verb *to experience* occurs till quite recently." Again: "Now, in the best English, *experience* is a substantive, *not a verb at all.*" *The Queen's English* (second ed.), pp. 115, 116, 252.

A person who can write thus has given an irresistible proof of his utter want of qualification to set up as a critic of English.

[2] In Dr. Latham's edition of Johnson's *Dictionary,* he would have found Bishop Thirlwall quoted for the verb *experience;* and the Bishop's authority is, certainly and deservedly, very high.

[3] Of the verb *experience* he gives two definitions, "to try, to practise", and "to know by practice". The first he is unable to exemplify; and, under the second, he confines himself to adducing Milton's "*experienced* eye", in which, if there were no verb *experience,* the epithet would be considered as an adjective. The positive existence of the verb thus rests upon the Doctor's bare

it.[1] In the eyes of Mr. White, however, it is a solecism which would soil any decent page. After having produced, with other supposed offenders, "an incensed farmer", real or imaginary, as "*experiencing* a cow", and two newspaper-writers, as "*experiencing* a climate" and "*experiencing* a hay-crop",[2] he thus concludes:

"Let us bear, suffer, try, live through, endure, prove, and undergo; and from all this we shall gain experience and become experienced; but let us not *experience* either a hay-crop, or a cow, or anything else."

How long we have possessed the verb *experience* I do not venture to say; but, as long ago as 1531, it was used by Sir Thomas Elyot;[3] in 1594, by Nash;[4] and, before the end of the sixteenth century, it had become familiar enough to find its way into a dictionary.[5] I suspect, however, that it had little currency prior to the time of the Commonwealth. First, apparently, it meant 'test', 'subject to experiment',[6] and then, 'know experimentally, or

assertion. His most inefficient editor, Archdeacon Todd, has nothing here to add to what he found.

[1] In the *Rambler* alone, he uses the verb *experience*, active or neuter, in Nos. 9, 16, 17, 35, 40, 42, 52, 63, 133, 184. Add the *Idler*, Nos. 2, 80; &c. &c.

[2] Inelegant as these expressions are, they have their parallels in writers of merit. Graves, the clever author of *The Spiritual Quixote*, makes *experience* govern "one fruitful season" and "one seasonable day". *Olla Podrida*, No. 30. Coleridge makes it govern "weather". *Essays on His Own Times*, p. 891. And Dr. Johnson, in his *Account of the Harleian Library*, makes it govern—I do not quote precisely as he wrote—"the use of a catalogue".

Every word is liable to be employed with bad taste; but it is no argument against it, that it is liable to such an employment.

[3] "And what utilytie should be acquired by suche declaration, it shoulde not be *experienced* with diligence?" *The Governour*, fol. 77.

[4] "No land can so infallibly *experience* the proverb 'The hood makes not the monk', as thou; for taylors, serving-men, make-shifts, and gentlemen, in thee are confounded." *Christ's Tears over Jerusalem*, p. 135 (in *Archaica*, Vol. 1).

Some years earlier, in his letter introductory to Greene's *Arcadia*, Nash uses the expression "in my *inexperienced* opinion". Gabriell Harvey, in his *Four Letters*, &c. (1592), has "*unexperienced* art".

In *Tarlton's Newes out of Purgatorie*, by an anonymous author, published in 1590, we find: "I presumed the rather to *experience*, with them, the hope of your favours." *Tarlton's Jests*, &c. (ed. Mr. J. O. Halliwell), p. 51.

[5] In Florio's *Worlde of Wordes* (ed. 1598), *sperimentare* is defined by "to trie, to proove, to *experience*, to put in practise."

[6] "It is an *experienced* proposition, that all things are loosned with the same cords wherewith they were bound." *Advertisements from Parnassus*, translated by Henry Earl of Monmouth (1656), p. 225.

from experience'. Richard Brathwait wrote, in 1640: "This, poore love-inthralled Mellida felt too well *experienc'd* in her."[1] The Earl of Monmouth, premising "irreverence towards God, disobedience of magistrates, corruption of manners, alteration of laws", and several other highly deprecable matters, adds: "many of which we, in the dominions of England, Scotland, and Ireland, have, of late, too sadly *experienced.*"[2] This was in 1654. Immediately afterwards, we have the authority of Milton[3] for the active *experience;* and, within the next thirty years, it was used by Matthew Lawrence,[4] Richard Franck,[5] Joseph Glanvill,[6] Dr. Henry More,[7] Richard Burthogge,[8] and Timothy Puller.[9]

Richard Franck has "to *experience* art". *Northern Memoirs* (ed. 1694), p. 55. Also see p. 105. This book was written, its author informs us, in 1658. There is an annotated edition of it by Sir Walter Scott.

In the first of these passages, *experienced*, passive, signifies 'which has passed the ordeal of experiment successfully'.

1 *The Two Lancashire Lovers* (1640), p. 128. "*Experienc'd* grounds of art", "*experienc'd* practises". *Ibid.*, pp. 225, 238. Also see *The English Gentleman, &c.* (ed. 1641), p. 7.

Richard Fleckno, whose authority, chronologically, is as good as that of anybody else, wrote, in 1647: "I shall be more happy than before, the more of unhappinesse I have *experienc'd* since." *A Relation of Ten Years Travells,* &c. (1655), p. 41. Another instance occurs at p. 93.

2 *The Compleat History of the Warrs of Flanders, The Translator's Epistle to his Countrymen, the Readers.* Also see the same translator's *Advertisements from Parnassus*, pp. 131, 151, 351.

3 "Besides, that your conspicuous piety and charity toward the orthodox, wherever overborne and oppressed, has been frequently *experienced* in the most urging straits and calamities of the churches." *Prose Works* (Bohn's ed.), Vol. 2, p. 254. Other instances occur in pp. 263, 267, of the first volume: they are, all, in letters, one of which bears the date of Jan., 1655. In two of these passages, *experience* may be taken to mean 'test'.

4 "When we *experience* the best ordinance sometimes empty, ... this will quicken us to look above," &c. *The Use and Practice of Faith* (1657), p. 330.

5 "The barble, though *experienced* a resolute fish," &c. *Northern Memoirs*, p. 274. Also see p. 60.

6 "But its *experienc'd* sterility through so many hundred years drives hope to desperation." *Scepsis Scientifica*, p. 133. Also see *Sadducismus Triumphatus*, p. 365.

7 "Such or such a configuration will have such an event, though they never *experienc'd* it at all, or very seldom." *Mystery of Godliness*, p. 359. Also see *Enthusiasmus Triumphatus* (ed. 1662), p. 45.

"But, it being *experienced*, of all hands, that the noise seemed to come from a force against the door," &c. Henry More, in Glanvill's *Sadducismus Triumphatus*, p. 437.

8 "Nothing is more obvious, or more frequently *experienced*, than this." *Causa Dei* (1675), p. 338.

9 "Christian moderation will govern any, when they have *experienced* an evil, not to run into the same again." *The Moderation of the Church of England* (1679), p. 317 (ed. 1843). Also see pp. 240, 294, 301, 309.

And already in the seventeenth century, *experience*, as a verb neuter,—since then grown very common, but not yet recognized by any dictionary,—was sanctioned by good writers.[1] Advancing to the eighteenth century, we encounter the active verb *experience* in Steele,[2] Bishop Berkeley,[3] &c. &c.;[4] and, still later, it has been used by Samuel

The following, from Shields, is quoted in *The Scotch Presbyterian Eloquence* (ed. 1693), p. 24: We have *experienced* wonders of the Lord's care," &c.

1 "We *experience* to the contrary." Franck's *Northern Memoirs*, p. 4.

"We *experience* that those objects occur to the mind tumultuously," &c. Thomas White, *An exclusion of Scepticks*, &c. (1665), p. 39. Also see p. 66.

Numerous references to the more modern writers could be given; but a few will, doubtless, be thought sufficient. Addison, *Guardian*, No. 157. Mandeville, *The Fable of the Bees* (ed. 1724), p. 330. Richardson, *Sir Charles Grandison*, Vol. 4, p. 128. Johnson, *Rambler*, No. 17. Mrs. Chapone, *Adventurer*, No. 78. Edward Moore, *World*, Nos. 2, 182. Earl of Cork, *Connoisseur*, No. 17. Gray, *Works*, Vol. 5, p. 199. Burke, *On the Sublime and Beautiful*, Part 1, Sect. 7. Cowper, *Works*, Vol. 6, p. 147. Southey, *Life of Wesley*, Vol. 2, p. 80. Coleridge, *Notes and Lectures upon Shakespeare*, &c., Vol. 2, pp. 149, 323.

2 *Guardian*, No. 148. While, in Queen Anne's time, the verb *experience* was not yet thoroughly in vogue, the verb *experiment*, for 'learn from experiment, or by experience', had not become obsolete. "This I have *experimented*, by taking away the grain which they looked for." Addison, *Guardian*, No. 156. It is, of course, a mere archaism in Burke's "*experimented* fidelity", and in Charles Lamb's Essay entitled *Popular Fallacies*.

3 *Guardian*, No. 27. Here occurs the passage quoted by Mr. White from Dr. Richardson's Dictionary.

4 Mandeville, *The Fable of the Bees*, p. 400. Aaron Hill, *Correspondence of Samuel Richardson*, Vol. 1, p. 92. For Richardson himself, see Vol. 2, p. 282, and Vol. 5, p. 6; for J. Channing, Vol. 2, p. 333. Richardson, *Sir Charles Grandison*, Vol. 1, pp. 228, 253, 294; Vol. 3, pp. 90, 116, 276, 357; Vol. 5, p. 179; Vol. 6, p. 17; Vol. 7, pp. 218, 246, 269. Hawkesworth, *Adventurer*, Nos. 5, 11, 33, 104. In Nos. 6, 77, 78, 79, are five other instances, by Bathurst and Mrs. Chapone. Sterne, *Sermons*, Nos. 24, 34, 39: *Letters*, Nos. 77, 91. Bishop Lowth, *Life of William of Wykeham*, p. 257. Henry Brooke, *The Fool of Quality* (ed. 1792), Vol. 1, p. 84; Vol. 3, p. 6; Vol. 4, p. 223; Vol. 5, pp. 89, 122, 260. Gray, *Works*, Vol. 3, p. 200; Vol. 4, p. 22: *Correspondence of Gray and Mason* (ed. 1855), p. 213. Foote, Dedication to *The Patron*. Shenstone, *Works* (ed. 1764), Vol. 2, p. 104: *Letters*, Nos. 17, 83, 90, 109. Kelly, *School for Wives*, Act 4, Scene 1. Charles Johnson, *Chrysal*, Vol. 1, pp. 124, 142; Vol. 2, pp. 190, 247; &c. &c. Miss Carter and Miss Talbot, in their letters to each other, use the verb *experience*, active and neuter, twenty-six times. Soame Jenyns, *World*, No. 178. Lord Chesterfield, *World*, Nos. 29, 98, 111. Edward Moore, in the same periodical, affords five instances; and there are others by W. Duncombe, Loveybond, &c. Burke, *On the Sublime and Beautiful*, Part 4, Sect. 17. I have remarked at least twenty instances in Burke's Speeches, Letters, &c. There are five instances in Miss Burney's *Evelina*. Robert Smith, *Microcosm*, Nos. 8, 20: also see Nos. 9, 27, 40, by various writers. Porson, *Tracts and Miscellaneous Criticisms*, p. 18. Bishop Horne, *Olla Podrida*, No. 13: also see Nos. 10, 20, 30, 32, 37, by Grose and others. In Paley's *Natural Theology* there are sixteen instances, of which seven are in a single chapter, the

Taylor Coleridge, Charles Lamb, Southey, Wordsworth, Shelley, Dr. Arnold, Mr. De Quincey, Lord Macaulay, Landor, Dr. Newman, Mr. Ruskin, and Mr. J. S. Mill.[1] The reader will not, I am sure, suppose that this list of references is cut short for want of available materials to extend it.

Some one writes, that an Armenian archbishop, having fallen among the savages of Abyssinia, "is *experiencing* very rough usage." Hereon Mr. White comments:

"He was *receiving* or *suffering* rough usage; and, although that was part of his *experience*, he did not *experience* it. *Experience* is the passing through a more or less continuous course of events or trials. A man's *experience* is the sum of his life; his *experience* in any profession, business, or condition of life, is the aggregate of the observation he has had the opportunity of making in that profession, business, or condition."

To the two last sentences there is no objection, if we read that "A man's *total experience* is the sum of his life"; [2] an amendment demanded by the definition given of *experience*. Moreover, that definition covers exactly what the Armenian

twenty-sixth. I have noticed eight instances in William Godwin's *Enquiry concerning Justice*. There are upwards of forty instances in the poet Cowper's letters alone.

[1] Coleridge, *Essays on His own Times*, pp. 314, 359, 396, 479, 823, 891: *Church and State*, &c., p. 274. Lamb, *Elia's Essays*, *Popular Fallacies: Letters*, Vol. 1, p. 135; Vol. 2, p. 285. Southey, *Letters*, &c. (1797), pp. 78, 271, 320: *Espriella's Letters*, Vol. 2, pp. 139, 393, 394; Vol. 2, pp. 103, 166, 311: *Life of Wesley* (ed. 1864), Vol. 1, pp. 139, 145, 208, 253; Vol. 2, pp. 33, 40, 146, 191, 212, 243, 248: *Colloquies*, &c., Vol. 1, p. 310; Vol. 2, pp. 117, 154, 398: *Essays, Moral and Political*, Vol. 1, pp. 52, 59, 131, 234, 293, 310, 373, 398, 417; Vol. 2, pp. 87, 126, 394: *Cowper's Works*, Vol. 1, p. 15; Vol. 2, pp. 9, 276; Vol. 3. p. 207. Wordsworth, *Concerning the Relations of Great Britain, Spain, and Portugal*, p. 94. Shelley, *Essays*, &c., Vol. 1, pp. 49, 50, 53, 60, 146, 165, 216, 262; Vol. 2, pp. 119, 170, 230: *Shelley Memorials*, p. 78. Dr. Arnold, *Life and Correspondence*, pp. 74, 223, 260, 299, 541. Mr. De Quincey, *Klosterheim*, pp. 88, 245: *Logic of Political Economy*, pp. 54, 153: *Works*, Vol. 16, pp. 81, 236, 365; &c. &c. Lord Macaulay, *Critical and Historical Essays* (ed. 1848), Vol. 1, pp. 139, 178, 243, 260, 350: *Speeches*, p. 75: *Miscellaneous Writings* (ed. 1860), Vol. 1, pp. 57, 88, 209, 219, 266, 267, 308; Vol. 2, pp. 99, 136, 239. These references might, probably, be doubled. *Experience*, the verb active, is found in the very first chapter of Lord Macaulay's *History*. Landor, *Last Fruit off an Old Tree*, pp. 6, 74, 128, 198, 317, 363: *Dry Sticks Fagoted*, pp. 78, 271, 320. Dr. Newman, *Essays, Critical and Historical*, Vol. 1, pp. 25, 47; Vol. 2, pp. 34, 228: *Discussions and Arguments on Various Subjects*, pp. 85, 310, 341, 387. Mr. Ruskin, *The Seven Lamps of Architecture*, p. 18. Mr. J. S. Mill, *On Liberty*, p. 23 (people's edition).

[2] If a man's *experience* be nothing less than "the sum of his life", Roger Ascham is nonsensical, with his "daylye *experience*" and "this *experience* of the wynde had I ones my selfe". *Toxophilus* (ed. 1868), pp. 152, 157.

archbishop was "passing through", namely, "a more or less continuous course of events or trials".[1] Of experiments, trials, proofs, observations, or of whatever incidents befall one, or come to one's knowledge, the more there are, the greater is one's resulting *experience;* yet, even from a single incident, information, or the like, we gain *experience.* If the issue is not *experience,* what is it? However crude its form, it is *experience;* and we have no more fitting name for it. As to the verb *experience,* there is, therefore, no case against it, on any ground whatsoever. Those who advisedly use it prefer it, as the Romans preferred *fungor,* because they wish to speak of a thing as a mere occurrence, or matter of observation, abstracted from passions and emotions. Lord Macaulay writes, in his biographical sketch of Bunyan: "With the pleasures, however, he *experienced* some of the pains, of eminence." Recast the sentence, and substitute, for *experienced,* 'enjoyed' and 'suffered'; the impression produced on the mind is altogether different, and that which Lord Macaulay advertently avoided conveying.

We are told, further:

> "From the noun *experience* is formed the participial adjective *experienced* (which is not the perfect participle of a verb *experience*), as *moneyed* from *money, landed* from *land, talented* from *talent, casemated* from *casemate, battlemented* from *battlement. Battlemented* is not a part of a verb, *I battlement, thou battlementest,* etc.; or *talented* from a verb, *I talent, thou talentest,* etc. So an *experienced* man is 'a man of experience', not 'one who has been experienced', i. e., according to the dictionaries, 'has been tried, proved, observed', but 'one who has tried, has proved, has observed'."

On the theory of Mr. White, *experienced,* as not being formed from a verb, has no more title than *bigoted* or *wretched* to the designation of "participial adjective", which

---

[1] Dean Alford is solicitous that the verb *experience,* if we must have it, should be "at least confined to its proper meaning, which is not simply to *feel,* but *to have personal knowledge of by trial";* and he objects to the expression "*experiences* a sensation". *The Queen's English,* p. 252. To this it is obvious to reply, that, to "feel" a sensation is impossible without "having personal knowledge of it by trial", unless it can be proved that there is such a thing as vicarious consciousness. The Dean might as well have urged, that, since we *see* a rose to be red, we may not say that we *know* it to be so.

he gives it. Also, since "a man's *experience* is the sum of his life", *experienced*, unqualified, can be used of himself by no man, with perfect safety, except at his last breath, and, so far forth, belongs, in all propriety, to the vocabulary of the next world. It is a simple assumption, too, that *experienced* "is not the perfect participle of a verb *experience*". Just as likely as not, it was preceded by the verb, as Dr. Johnson and others suppose it to have been; and, in the absence of evidence, Mr. White is precisely as blamable for precipitation as the lexicographers. These, however, if we grant their premises, are not so insensate as Mr. White hastily takes them to be, in deducing *experienced*, to mean 'who *has experienced*', from a verb active.[1] We understand, by a *learned* man, a man 'who *has learned*' many things, not one 'who *has been learned*'; and, by a *dissipated* man, a man 'who *has dissipated*' something, not one 'who has *been dissipated*', or squandered. An *affected* coxcomb *affects* something; a *determined* ruffian *determines* something: they are not objects, but subjects, of affectation and determination. *Sworn* enemies *have sworn* mutual enmity; *perjured* witnesses *have perjured* themselves.[2] Should it turn out—and I dare say it will,—that *experience*, as a verb neuter,[3] was in use before *experienced*, an *experienced* man has its parallels in *retired* statesman, *coalesced* monarchs, *wonted* manner, *mistaken* eulogist, *departed* joys, *expired* lease, *escaped* convict, *apostatized* church, *decayed* cheesemonger, *relapsed* heretic, *rotten* apple, and *fallen* angel.

"Perhaps an objection to the use of this word as a verb has no better ground than that of taste or individual preference, which should be excluded from discussions like the present; yet I am inclined to make that objection very strongly." In these terms Mr. White opens his tirade against the verb *experience*. Contrasted with

---

[1] *Expertus*, like *experienced*, signifies both 'knowing by experience' and 'known by experience'. 'Un médécin fort *experimenté*' is 'a very *experienced* physician', though *experimenter* is 'to test', 'to put to trial'. From *sperimentare* and *spermentare* come *sperimentato* and *spermentato*, denoting alike 'provato' and 'che ha esperienza'.

[2] Our old *seen* sometimes meant 'versed'; and I might remark on *versed*, *versé*, *versatus*.

[3] Why do our dictionaries still give *aged* as an adjective, unless it be indubitably settled to be older than the verb neuter *age*?

scientific deduction, opinion, in the quaint phrase of Landor, is "like an empty egg-shell in a duck-pond, turned on its stagnant water by the slightest breath of air; at one moment the crackt side nearer to sight, at another the sounder, but the emptiness at all times visible."

And now the reader may decide for himself, as between Dean Alford and Mr. White, whose talent, with regard to his treatment of the verb *experience*, is the more heroic, that of the former, for assertion, or that of the latter, for sequacity; the ignorance of the two being equal.

Mr. White's remarks on a perfectly classical use of *commence* here follow, unabridged:

> "There is a British misuse of this word which is remarkably coarse and careless. British writers of all grades but the very highest will say, for instance, that a man went to London and *commenced* poet, or *commenced* politician. Mr. Swinburne says that 'Blake *commenced* pupil'; and Pope, quoted by Johnson:
>
> 'If wit so much from ignorance undergo,
> Ah, let not learning, too, *commence* its foe.'
>
> A man may *commence* life, as an author, or a politician, or he may *commence* a book, or any other task, although it is better to say he *begins* either.[1] But it is either a state or an action that he *commences*. *Commencement* cannot be properly predicated of a noun which does not express the idea of continuance. It may be said that a woman *commences* married life, or that she *commences* jilting, but not that she *commences* wife, or *commences* jilt, any more than that she *ends* hussy."

Clearly, a person who criticizes in this way must look upon *commence*, for 'begin to be', 'become', 'set up as', or the like,[2] as having little justification, so far as justification is determinable by the usage of good writers.[3] Yet it has been employed by first-class authorities for more than two centuries.[4] Generally, it is followed immedi-

[1] How is it, then, that we find, in Mr. White's *Life and Genius of Shakespeare*, pp. 77, 111, "to *commence* his studies" and "to *commence* a suit"?

[2] Dr. Johnson, in his *Life of Swift*, writes: "He seems desirous enough of *recommencing* courtier". *Recommence*, as here, for 'begin anew to be', is unnoticed by the lexicographers.

[3] The use of *commence* here spoken of is not registered in Dr. Richardson's *Dictionary*.

[4] "Young scholars . . . *commence* schoolmasters in the country". Fuller, *The Holy State and the Profane State* (1642), p. 99 (ed. 1841). — "For,

ately by a substantive; but Budgell, Richardson, Gray, Dr. Johnson, Hawkesworth, Shenstone, and Cowper, in some of the passages referred to below, interpose the indefinite article.[1] In rare cases, it is followed by an adjective.[2]

For any peculiar elegance in the use of *commence* which

---

shall . . . man . . . not, whilst living here, *commence* angel, in his holy and heavenly affections?": *Id.*, *Good Thoughts in Worse Times* (1647), *Occasional Meditations*, VIII. Milton, in his title "Accedence *commenced* Grammar." Congreve, Epistle Dedicatory to *The Double Dealer*. *The Scotch Presbyterian Eloquence*, p. 18. Steele, *Tatler*, Nos. 19, 187: *Spectator*, No. 172: *Guardian*, Nos. 17, 87. Budgell, *Spectator*, No. 150. Hughes, *Spectator*, No. 525. Mandeville, *Fable of the Bees*, p. 87. De Foe, *Political History of the Devil*, pp. 25, 27, 40, 69, 88, 184, 254, 295, 356. Bishop Lavington, *Enthusiasm of Methodists and Papists Compared* (ed. 1833), p. 183. Richardson, *Clarissa Harlowe*, Vol. 8, p. 189: *Pamela* (ed. 1811), Vol. 2, p. 279: *Correspondence*, Vol. 2, p. 106. Murphy, *All in the Wrong*, Act 3, Scene 1. Bickerstaffe, *Love in a Village*, Act 1, Scene 1. Foote, *The Commissary*, Act 1, Scene 1. Gray, *Works*, Vol. 4, p. 109. Horace Walpole, *World*, No. 160: in the same periodical, in Nos. 40, 57, 133, 182, by Edward Moore, there are instances; and others, in Nos. 38, 66, 86, 147, 193, by Parratt, Anon., Cole, Sir David Dalrymple, and Tilson. Dr. Johnson, *Rambler*, Nos. 1, 93, 116, 179, 182: *Adventurer*, No. 102: *London*: *Life of Sydenham*: *Life of Ascham*: *Journey to the Western Islands of Scotland*: *Lives of the English Poets*, Milton, Otway, Dryden, Sprat, Prior, Blackmore, Savage, Swift, Akenside. Dr. Joseph Warton, *Adventurer*, No. 129. Hawkesworth, *Adventurer*, No. 13. William Shenstone, *Works*, Vol. 2, pp. 3, 161, 168, 224: *Letters*, No. 8. George Colman, *The Comedies of Terence, translated*, &c. (ed. 1810), p. 420: also see, in the *Connoisseur*, by Colman and Thornton jointly, Nos. 6, 24, 48, 92, 106, 109, 116; and Nos. 82, 104, by Anon. Charles Johnson, *Chrysal*, Vol. 2, pp. 249, 274; Vol. 3, pp. 90, 253; Vol. 4, p. 42. Henry Brooke, *The Fool of Quality*, Vol. 5, p. 84. Horne Tooke, in *Junius's Letters*, No. 53. Gibbon, in a letter to Mr. Holroyd, Feb. 21, 1772. Cowper, *Works*, Vol. 2, pp. 204, 218, 223, 237. I have counted seventeen instances in Cowper's prose alone. Also see his *Odyssey*, 18, 431. George Canning, *Microcosm*, Nos. 2, 7. Bishop Horne and Kett, *Olla Podrida*, Nos. 23, 27. Jones, of Nayland, *Theological and Miscellaneous Works*, Vol. 5, p. 415; Vol. 6, p. 39. Charles Lamb, *Final Memorials*, &c., Vol. 1, pp. 66, 219: *Elia's Essays*, *On the Danger of Confounding Moral with Personal Deformity*. Hazlitt, *Lectures on the English Comic Writers* (ed. 1841), pp. 190, 345: *Table-talk* (ed. 1846), Vol. 2, pp. 47, 65. Southey, *Annual Review*, Vol. 3, p. 492: *Quarterly Review*, Vol. 16, p. 227; Vol. 27, p. 2: *Life of Wesley*, Vol. 2, pp. 157, 159: *Colloquies*, &c., Vol. 2, p. 86: *Cowper's Works*, Vol. 1, pp. 78, 195; Vol. 2, pp. 12, 169: *The Doctor* (monotome ed.), p. 33. I might also refer largely to Southey's letters, &c. &c. Coleridge, *Notes and Lectures upon Shakespeare*, Vol. 1, p. 88. Mr. De Quincey, *Works*, Vol. 5, p. 78; Vol. 11, p. 115. Mr. Keble, *Hooker's Works* (ed. 1841), Preface, p. xlviii.

[1] Colman and Thornton once interpose the definite article, in "*commence* the fine gentlemen". *Connoisseur*, No. 48.

[2] "*Commence* eternal". Steele, *Tatler*, No. 187. "If any man should be enticed to follow him, he, too, is thenceforward to *commence* infallible". Jones, of Nayland, *Theological and Miscellaneous Works*, Vol. 1, p. 145.

Mr. White scouts so contemptuously I do not contend; but the locution, far from being "remarkably coarse and careless", is perfectly unexceptionable; and I should be surprised, if any one else had ever before found fault with it.[1] Nor has "*commences* wife" a parallel in "*ends* hussy", in which expression, moreover, there is nothing to blame but curt ruggedness.[2] In order to their parallelism, "*commences* wife" should signify 'begins *with being* a wife', a very different thing from 'begins *to be* a wife'; even as the nature of an appearance and the fact of an appearance are not identical.[3] By way of proving the absurdity of "*commences* wife", we are instructed that "*commencement* cannot be properly predicated of a noun which does not express the idea of continuance". We are forbidden, then, to say that a boy '*commences* the rule-of-three'; the idea of continuance not being expressed by the mathematical operation. What Mr. White fails to see is, that the phrases he is dealing with are elliptical.[4] He might as well argue

---

[1] "To *commence* M.A.", &c., meaning 'to take the degree of M.A.', &c., has been a recognized phrase for some three centuries, at least. "Thei were able to have *commenced maisters of arte*." Barnabe Riche, *Farewell to Militarie Profession*, p. 45. This application of *commence* probably originated in an imitation of *incipere*, which, in modern Latin, has long been used to denote the object of college-commencements; and it is not at all unlikely that it suggested the extension of employment which the term has obtained in ordinary discourse. See Mr. B. H. Hall's *College Words and Customs* (2nd ed.), p. 85.

As equivalent to *commence* M.A., &c., *proceed* is very common in literature.

[2] "They may *begin* censors, and be obliged to *end* accomplices." Burke, *Speech on Mr. Fox's East-India Bill*, near the end.

The following is also in point: "Every affection is, by nature, a short fury, which, if it growe vehement, and become habituall, *concludes* madnesse." Sir Arthur Gorges, Translation of Bacon's *De Sapientia Veterum* (ed. 1619), p. 114.

[3] I can, however, produce an instance of *commence* in the sense of 'begin with being'. "Our divinity, like the grandfather of humanity, was born in the fulness of time, and in the strength of its manly vigour; but philosophy and arts *commenced* embryos, and are, by times, gradual accomplishments." Glanvill, *Scepsis Scientifica*, p. 140.

Still more unidiomatic is the use of *commence* in the following sentence: "But yet this is so difficult in the impartial and exact performance, that it may be well reckon'd among the bare possibilities which never *commence* into a futurity." *Id.*, *ibid.*, p. 56.

[4] This lands me, I know, in the conclusion that "*commences* poet" is for '*commences to be* poet', which is hardly English, save to Scotchmen and such-like. See Mr. Marsh's *Lectures on the English Language*, p. 183, foot-note. But equally alien to our idiom is 'I *will to* say', into which, however, we must explain 'I *will* say'. This and "*commences* poet" are alike conventional.

against '*walking* the streets', '*rowing* a race', '*running* riot,' '*trotting* a mile', '*going* a circuit', or '*sitting* a horse'; or contend that we have a verb active in "the moon *showed* purple".

By "a British misuse" of a word he means, in the present instance, a use of it which he does not know to be sanctioned by many of the best English writers;[1] just as some other American might carp at *hustings*, or at *firing*, for 'fuel', if uninformed of their long-standing currency in the mother-country. That, from meagreness of literature, badness of memory, or whatever other cause, he could put forth the paragraph which has been transcribed is hardly consistent with his possessing those specific qualifications which we expect in one who would teach others English. And his cogency of reasoning tallies harmoniously with his knowledge of documentary authority. Let his style of argumentation be imitated, in application to *turn*, for 'become'. "This use, contemplated abstractedly, is utterly preposterous. We may say that a man *turns* a pancake, or *turns* his back, but not that he *turns* traveller, any more than that he *returns* beggar."

Mr White, though he frowns severely upon *telegram*, has not the remotest conception why the learned hold it to be wrong. This I shall prove presently, when I quote his observations on the obnoxious vocable. In the mean time I rehearse the argument on which it has been condemned by scholars. And here the reader is duly forewarned to make short work of the next few pages, unless he would be reminded of dryness compared with which that of "the remainder-biscuit after a voyage" will be voted succulence itself.

In devising a legitimate Greek substantive of the complex order, we are, first, to consider whether, by the analogy of the Greek language, the idea awaiting expression should be represented by a compound, or by a de-

---

[1] Mr. White is altogether a critic after the fashion of M. Francis Wey, who thus treats the word *paupérisme:* "Un vilain mot! c'est la pauvreté en général, devenue l'objet d'un système, et exploitée comme objet de spéculation. . . Les Anglais, qui nous ont donné ce mot, étaient bien dignes de l'inventer . . . Ce mot est un produit du *socialisme* qui s'est glissé de notre temps dans les sciences morales, à l'ombre de la philosophie du dernier siècle." *Rémarques sur la Langue Française*, etc., Vol. 1, p. 196.

rivative; a verb being, indispensably, the proximate base on which we operate.[1] A person or thing that acts, &c.,[2] is expressible, generally, among complex formatives, by a compound; but the abstract action, &c., of such person or thing, and likewise the result of an action, demand derivatives, absolutely.

Further, a verb can, properly, be compounded with no part of speech but a preposition; in which case, the two words are simply yoked, unchanged, together.[3] A verb in which the first element is a substantive or adverb is not compound, but derivative; it being educed from some preexistent compound substantive.

To obtain a term meaning 'the result of writing at a distance', 'that which is telegraphed', taking *τῆλε* and *γράφω*, we must, to begin, construct the synthetic compound *τηλέγραφος*,[4] substantive and adjective, of which the masculine might denote 'a person who writes at a distance', and the masculine or neuter, 'an instrument for writing at a distance'. Compare *λιθοβόλος*, 'hurler of stones', 'stone-hurling', and this, or *λιθοβόλον*, 'an engine for hurling stones'.

Having reached *τηλέγραφος*, the next step is to form a verb from it; and its verb must be *τηλεγραφέω*,[5] 'to write

---

[1] Originally it was the substantive, and that a simple, which led. *Φιλία* came from *φιλέω*; but that came from *φίλος*.

[2] Here and just below, I refer, by '&c.', to substantives educed from verbs neuter and passive.

For simplicity, I confine myself, in speaking of compounds, to those consisting of only two members each.

[3] In *κυνόσουρα*, *ναυσικλυτός*, &c., there is, also, mere contact of words; but none of them has a verb as a constituent.

Among Greek compounds,—in their exhaustive distribution into parathetic, synthetic, and a transitional class thereto intermediate,—the parathetic are inorganic, and are resoluble into independent words; while the synthetic are organic, and, being made up of constituents modified, more or less, with a view to combination, are not thus resoluble.

In English, *overpass*, *priestcraft*, and *bridesmaid* are parathetics; *gossip*, *grandam*, *hussy*, *nostril*, *sheriff*, and *stalwart* are synthetics. *Belman*, *brimstone*, *fortnight*, *gospel*, *sennight*, *shepherd*, *wisdom*, *worship* are synthetic only in part. Phonic synthetics we have in abundance; as *boatswain*, *breakfast*, *forehead*, *housewife*, *rowlock*, *twopence*, *vineyard*.

[4] This compound, like all its kindred, is incapable of resolution into substantive words; for *γραφος*, *γραφια*, *γραφεω*, *γραφημα*, and *γραφησις* are nothing by themselves. And so it is with the *γραμματον* of *τηλεγράμματον*. Nor have we, in *τηλεγραφικός*, *τῆλε* + *γραφικός*, but a development of *τηλέγραφος*.

[5] From *τηλεγραφέω*, like *τηλεβολέω*, we get, also, *τηλεγραφία*, 'the act or art of writing at a distance', 'telegraphy'. Compare *λιθοβολία*. As a

at a distance'; the barytone τηλεγράφω [1] being unprecedented. From this we develop τηλεγράφημα; as ζωγράφημα, φιλοσόφημα, and χειρογράφημα are developed from ζωγραφέω, φιλοσοφέω, and χειρογραφέω. As its synonym, we might have τηλέγραφον,[2] the passive.

The words τηλέγραφος and τηλέγραφον might shorten, to become English, into *telegraph;* but then, if we accepted all their possible Greek senses, we should have one word for 'sender of a message', 'the instrument that conveys the message', and 'the message sent'. [3] Consonantly to rule, 'the message sent' would also be expressed by *telegrapheme.* *Telegram,* however convenient, is, from a philological point of view, a malformation.[4]

---

synonym of τηλεγραφία, we might coin τηλεγράφησις, on the model of οἰκοδόμησις and φιλοποίησις. After τηλέγραφος come τηλεγραφικός, &c.

From τηλεγραφέω might, further, be educed τηλεγράφης, equivalent to τηλέγραφος, 'telegrapher'. Compare γεωμέτρης.

[1] If there could be such a verb, it might have, as a derivative, τηλέγραμμα. But τηλέγραμμα, if possible as a compound of τῆλε and γράμμα, could signify only some such thing as 'a letter at a distance'. So, ἐπίγραμμα, ἐπιγραφή, &c., if compounds, would not mean what they do, but 'on-letter', 'on-figure', &c., or the like: they would want the force which they possess as being derived from compound verbs and denoting their results. In δίγαμμα and Δύσπαρις there is no constituent allied to verbs.

The only substantive nearly resembling, in appearance, τηλέγραμμα that could be formed is the adjectival τηλέγραμμον, from γραμμή; and it would mean 'that which consists of distant lines', &c. Its English form, would be *telegram.* Compare *parallelogram.*

Τηλεγράμματον, a neuter substantive from τηλεγράμματος, would have the sense of 'that which has letters at a distance', or 'that which has letters wide asunder'. Compare μονογράμματον and τηλέπυλον.

[2] Since the word begins with an adverb, the accent of the active derivative and that of the passive derivative are the same, that is to say, proparoxytone. Mr. Farrar—see note [4], below,—in writing τηλεγράφος, misplaces his accent.

[3] The French *photographe* means both 'photograph' and 'photographer'; and *lithographe* has, likewise, a double function.

[4] *Telegram* has been discussed, though not very perspicuously, by Dr. Donaldson, in the last edition of his *New Cratylus.*

The Rev. F. W. Farrar, in his *Brief Greek Syntax* (ed. 1870), p. 53, after stating that abstract substantives like λιθοβολή, ναυμάχη, &c., would be at war with rule, goes on, with a "hence", to cashier *telegram.* As this is a concrete substantive, it is inscrutable how Mr. Farrar works out its condemnation.

Telegram, to Mr. Farrar, is "a monstrosity", and, in words which he quotes anonymously, "a spot of barbarity impressed so deep on the English language, that criticism never can wash it away". Yet, no better is our everyday *dilemma,* which no one scruples at. For δίλημμα can only most improbably be accounted an arbitrary syncopation of διάλημμα; and the existence of διλήμματον seems to show that it was not accounted to be such. It is interesting that we find it in bad Latin long before we find it in still worse Greek.

Of *telegram* Mr. White discourses as follows: [1]

"This word, which is claimed as an 'American' production, has taken root quickly, and is, probably, well fixed in the language. It is both superfluous and incorrectly formed; but it is regarded as convenient, and has been allowed to pass muster. *Telegraph* is equally good as a verb expressing the act of writing, and as a noun expressing the thing written. This is according to a well-known analogy of the language. But they who must have a distinct etymology for every word may regard *telegraph*, the verb, as from γραφειν (*graphein*) = 'to write'; and the noun as from the Greek noun γραφη (*graphé*) = 'a writing'. In *monograph*, *epigraph*, and *paragraph*, the last syllable, in like manner, represents γραφη (*graphé*); in *monogram*, *epigram*, and *diagram*, the last syllable represents γραμμα (*gramma*) = 'an engraved character', 'a letter'. This distinction, remembered, will prevent a confusion which prevails, with many speakers, as to certain words in *graph* and *gram*. A *monograph* is an essay or an account having a single subject; a *monogram*, a character or cipher composed of several letters combined in one figure: an *epigraph* is an inscription, a citation, a motto; an *epigram*, a

---

No fewer than twelve letters on *telegram* appeared in *The Times* newspaper during the month of October, 1857. Fierce was the controversy waged thereupon between the two great English Universities. As a learned friend remarks to me, "It is a nineteenth-century parallel to the Phalaris dispute between Bentley and the Oxonians. All the insolence is on their side, and all the ignorance, also."

But even those who contended that *telegrapheme* was, analogically, the right word felt it to be insupportable for any but holiday use. F, in *The Times* of October 23, 1857, proposes recourse to τῆλε and πέμπω, whence *telepomp*, to be shortened into *pump!*

The armoury to which all scholars have been indebted for their weapons against *telegram* is the Parerga appended to Lobeck's edition of Phrynichus. For an opportunity of studying Lobeck's own words, I am beholden to the kindness of my friend, Mr. E. B. Cowell, Professor of Sanskrit in the University of Cambridge; and I have also to thank him for several valuable hints, and solutions of my doubts.

[1] Instead of the second sentence of the passage here copied, we learn, at pp. 416, 420, that Mr. White first wrote: "It is convenient, and is correctly enough formed to pass muster." This was understood, by a critic, as indicating ignorance that *telegram* is "altogether an incorrect formation"; and Mr. White's reply is: "I have mistaken the force of my language, if it did not convey to my readers, every one of them, that, in my judgment, *telegram* is an incorrectly formed word, but that the irregularity is of a kind not worth making a point about." Why, then, has he persisted in making a point about it? And, especially, why has he changed his language? He can only say, that calling a word, without qualification, "incorrectly formed" is simply a better way of expressing the opinion that it is "correctly enough formed to pass muster". It is the fact that *telegram* has been generally adopted, and it is this consideration alone, that legitimates it.

short poem on one subject. The confusion of these terminations has recently led some writers into errors which are amazing and amusing. We have had *photogram* proposed, and *stereogram*, and—Cadmus save us!—*cablegram*, not only proposed, but used. . . . The first two, although homogeneous, are incorrect; the proper termination, in both cases, being *graph*, representing *γραφη* (*graphé*), 'a writing', and not *gram*, from *γραμμα* (*gramma*), 'a character'."

That Mr White believes the legitimacy or illegitimacy of *telegram* to be ascertainable by his most unscholastic method of procedure affords a very conclusive criterion of his pretensions as a philologist. He turns up the words *γραφή* and *γράμμα* in "Hederici Lexicon", which he learnedly quotes, no doubt to the same effect that was produced by the grandiloquence of Goldsmith's village-schoolmaster; these substantives, he discovers, signify, respectively, "a writing" and "an engraved character, a letter"; he defines certain familiar English words in *-graph* and *-gram*; and, as, on comparison with these words, *telegram* ought, he implies, to denote some sort of "engraved character" or "letter", he concludes it to be, in the sense which we attach to it, a misnomer. The word, as to formation, is, to him, all well enough; only we give it a wrong signification, and have introduced, in it, a superfluous synonym. To his thinking, moreover, it is a compound; whereas it is an unlicensed derivative.[1]

Our words in *-graph* and *-gram*, so far as they conform to Mr. White's canon, conform to it by sheer fortuity; and accidents are a sorry basis on which to found a principle. But where did he learn the existence of the impossible *μονογραφή* and *μονόγραμμα*, as the originals of our *monograph* and *monogram*?[2] How, too, are we to dispose

---

[1] See note [1] to p. 43.

[2] *Monograph* is a lawful compound, if referred to *μονόγραφον*, which might have been Greek. But *monogram*, with reference to its acceptation, connecting it with *γράμμα*, stands on the same footing, etymologically, with *telegram*. Shortened from *μονόγραμμον*, a real word, it would come from *γραμμή*, and its sense would be 'outline', 'sketch'. The Greek word which we moderns should have gone to is *μονογράμματον*, for which, in a unique instance in corrupt Greek, *μονόγραμμον* is found substituted. Like *μονόγραμμον* is the *didrachma* of modern numismatologists; the Greek word, from *δραχμή*, being *δίδραχμον*.

Several of our lawless formations in *-graph* and *-gram* were first suggested in France; and *telegram*, it is said, is one of them.

of *digraph* and *digram*,—both of them like *telegram*, as to structure,—between the senses of which no distinction is observed? A rule to serve the purpose of that so summarily formulated for us could be good for nothing, at least to try neoterisms by, unless it were deduced from an examination of Greek words as they were used by the Greeks; and, even after such an examination, a person unacquainted with the laws of verbal composition and derivation in Greek could by no possibility escape disastrous miscarriage, if called to sit in judgment on *telegram*.

In Greek, the difference between *ἐπιγραφή* and *ἐπίγραμμα*, as that between *διαγραφή* and *διάγραμμα*, *συγγραφή* and *σύγγραμμα*, *παραγραφή* and *παράγραμμα*, *ἀναγραφή* and *ἀνάγραμμα*, is matter of convention; the three first pairs are, sometimes, even used synonymously; in scarcely one of them can we trace, through its -*γραμμα*, reference to "an engraved character, a letter"; and, in such of these words as contain -*γραφη*, 'the act of writing' is pointed to, primarily, rather than "a writing". Besides, what would Mr. White do with *autograph*, *chirograph*, and *holograph*, the Greek originals of which do not end in -*γραφη*? Or with *parallelogram*, the Greek original of which does not end in -*γραμμα*?[1] Or with *program*,[2] the -*gram* of which no more than that of *epigram* and *diagram* supports his rule by its signification?[3]

---

[1] Παραλληλόγραμμον is the Greek original of *parallelogram*.

[2] So I spell purposely. If others would rather have *programme*, *christianise*, &c. &c., be it so. By the time we get back to *baptising*, we shall again be very fair sham Frenchmen.

[3] Mr. Marsh says, of *telegram*, that, "in spite of the objections of some Hellenists against it, as an anomalous formation, the English ear is too familiar with Greek compounds of the same elements, to find this word repugnant to our own principles of etymology." *Lectures on the English Language*, p. 280.

This may well mortify us, seeing whom it comes from. So indifferent a Grecian, it appears, is Mr. Marsh, as to think that *telegram* is not demonstrably past all philological defence. And is "the English ear", irrespectively of scholastic cultivation, to be allowed to dictate "our own principles of etymology" for us?

Dr. Worcester, in his Dictionary, and Dr. Webster's editors, in theirs, quote, with silent approval, the subjoined ignorant vindication of *telegram*: "The word is formed according to the strictest laws of the language from which its root comes. *Telegraph* means 'to write from a distance'; *telegram*, 'the writing itself, executed from a distance'. *Monogram*, *logogram*, &c., are words formed on the same analogy, and in good acceptation."

Professor Schele De Vere, in the present year, has asserted that *telegram* is

"They who must have a distinct etymology for every word" are apprised, by Mr. White, with the condescending benevolence of a good-natured oracle, that they may regard the verb *telegraph* as from γράφειν, and the substantive *telegraph* as from γραφή. As one may not suspect that he teaches what he does not himself believe, it follows, from this, that he thinks we have only to affix γράφειν to τῆλε, in order to make a good Greek verb on which to father our English verb; and that τῆλε and γραφή, combined, would give τηλεγραφή,[1] as the source of our substantive *telegraph*. Yet τηλεγράφειν and τηλεγραφή are, both, impossible. To match his synthesis of τῆλε and γραφή into τηλεγραφή, τηλέγραφος would yield, on analysis, τῆλε and γράφος. In like manner, the last member of *pacificus* would be *ficus;* an etymology to be valued literally at a fig. Further, Mr. White might easily have found out, as an historical fact, that our substantive *telegraph* preceded our verb *telegraph,* and led to it.

For the same futile reason, turning on the meaning of *-gram,* which he brings against *telegram,* he condemns *photogram* and *stereogram.* To convey their current meanings, they are indefensible, certainly. To prove them so, I should have to add but little to what I have already written; and I need not dwell on them as hypothetically referable to φωτόγραμμον and στερεόγραμμον.

But enough. Yet, tedious as is all this circumstantiality, it will not fail of its design, if it but serves to impress the wholesome lesson, that a man who meddles with a subject beyond his competency may look for confusion rather than for increase of reputation. Besides, it is high time that I should turn to the introductory pages of the volume under review. Open the volume, however, where one may, every new paragraph, as one reads on, contributes something to alienate a predisposition to confidence, and furnishes its contingent of specific evidence in cumulation towards an unfavourable final verdict.

"formed after the analogy of *epigram* and *monogram,* to distinguish the result of the process of telegraphing from the instrument." *Americanisms,* p. 559. At p. 488, this gentleman writes of "ἐλέγη", as the original of our *elegy.* Plainly, his Greek, and so Mr. Grant White's, is of a stamp which would have appeared a novelty to Bentley or Porson.

[1] So M. Littré takes *télégramme* from τῆλε and γράμμα.

A letter to Mr. J. R. Lowell, with which Mr. White auspicates his book, opens thus:

"When your forefather met mine, as he probably did, some two hundred and thirty or forty years ago, in the newly laid out street of Cambridge (and there is reason for believing that the meeting was likely to be about where Gore Hall now stands)," &c.

The very first line excited my suspicions. But I pass to the parenthesis. The likelihood as to the place of the meeting hypothesized is a question of the present time; and the meeting itself is referred to the past. "Was likely to be" must, therefore, be altered to 'is likely to have been'. Again, "reason for believing" is simply a circumlocution for what is 'likely';[1] and, hence, the words are superfluous, unless Mr. White would be understood as intending the likelihood of a likelihood.

Let us now turn to page 5 of the Preface. There we read: "A case in point—trifling and amusing, but not, therefore, less suggestive,—recently attracted my attention". Almost as much as by the words 'but, therefore, not less suggestive', it is here notified, that the case in point, inasmuch as it is trifling and amusing, is no less suggestive than it would be, if otherwise; as if a thing were suggestive in proportion to its triviality and amusingness. But Mr. White purposed to convey the idea, that its being trifling and amusing does not detract from its suggestiveness. Accordingly, he ought to have put, instead of "therefore", 'for all that', and after the "not", or before it, indifferently.[2] Further down the page, we find the expression "to *make* a visit", which, whatever it once was, no longer is English; and also *parlour*, for 'drawing-room', a sense which, except in the United States and in some of the English Colonies, is obsolete.

In so severe and scornful a critic as Mr. White we have a right to count on a knowledge of common vernacular English; but there is not a little which the teacher himself still has to be taught. At p. 51, he pronounces *would*

---

[1] One of Dr. Johnson's definitions of *likely* is, "such as may, in reason, be thought or believed."

[2] Sentences containing *therefore* as here used by Mr. White, and also *on that account*, might be adduced, I know, from classical writers. But one man's carelessness is no plea for another man's.

and *which* to be "test-words as to the mastery of idiom".[1] Yet, in his very first page, we read:

"This conclusion, be it new or old, is sound; but it would be very weak reasoning that *would* draw, from the fact that language is formed, on the whole, by consent and custom, an argument in favour of indifference as to the right or wrong of usage."

Of course, the right word, in lieu of that which I have italicized, is *should*.[2] We find, too, at p. 65:

"A man who *would* write well without training, would write, not more clearly or with more strength, but with more elegance, if he were educated."

Again, adverting to a dissertation by Addison, he writes, at p. 70:

"But he manifestly intended to say, that he *would* use the words 'imagination' and 'fancy' promiscuously."

Once more, at p. 269, having quoted the perfectly idiomatic "it was requested that no persons *would* leave their seats during dinner", he adds this absurd comment:

"Here the right word is *should*; as *would* and *should* follow the regimen of *will* and *shall*; and we request that people *shall* do thus or so, not that they *will* do it".

Most assuredly, unless the English of Edinburgh, Dublin, and New York be accepted as our standard,[3] we do no

---

[1] It would be curious to have Mr. White's opinion as to how *which* is used by masters of idiom. Why has he withheld it?

[2] "A man would be laugh'd at by most people, who *should* maintain that too much money could undo a nation." Mandeville, *Fable of the Bees*, p. 213.

"A concussion that *should* shatter the pyramid would threaten the dissolution of the continent." Johnson, *Rasselas*, Chapter 31.

"A country in which places of dignity and confidence *should* cease to be at the disposal of faction, favour, and interest, would not long be the residence of servility and deceit." Godwin, *An Enquiry concerning Political Justice*, Book 1, chapter 4.

"That man would do a great and permanent service to the ministry, who *should* publish a catalogue of the books in history", &c. &c. Southey, *Life of Wesley*, Vol. 1, p. 309, foot-note.

[3] For a profound discussion of *shall* and *will*, *should* and *would*, see Dr. Shadworth H. Hodgson's *Theory of Practice*, Vol. 2, Chap. 4, Para. 22.

"Not one Londoner in ten thousand can lay down the rules for the proper use of *will* and *shall*. Yet not one Londoner in a million ever misplaces his *will* and *shall*. Doctor Robertson could, undoubtedly, have written a luminous dissertation on the use of those words. Yet, even in his latest work, he sometimes misplaced them ludicrously." So writes Lord Macaulay. Mr. White has not done what Doctor Robertson perhaps could have done; but,

4

such thing.[1] Neither in Old England nor in New is there a plough-boy of ten years old that could not here set Mr. White right, his proud talk about "mastery of idiom" to the contrary notwithstanding. And, as in these instances, so it falls out, not unfrequently, that he is

"Most confident, when palpably most wrong."

Nor is he more fortunate as relates to pronunciation. "It may here be pertinently remarked, that the pronunciation of *a* in such words as *glass, last, father,* and *pastor* is a test of high culture".[2] Uncultivated persons, he goes on to say, are apt to give the *a* of these words "the thick, throaty sound of *aw*", or else the sound of the vowel in *an* and *at*. He concludes:

"Next to that tone of voice which, it would seem, is not to be acquired by any striving in adult years, and which indicates breeding rather than education, the full, free, unconscious utterance of the broad *ah* sound of *a* is the surest indication, in speech, of social culture which began at the cradle".

But "the broad *ah* sound of *a*" may be out of season as well as in season. *Glass, last,* and *pastor*, with their *a* sounded, to satisfy Mr. White's sense of politeness, like that in *father*, come perilously near being vulgarisms.[3]

like the Doctor, he has practically shown that a man who is unaccustomed to hear *will* and *shall* rightly distinguished by the people about him is pretty certain to blunder with his neighbours.

Cobbett, in his *English Grammar*, § 258, speaking of the uses of *shall, will, should, would,* &c., calls them uses which, "various as they are, are as well known to us as the uses of our teeth and noses; and to misapply which words argues not only a deficiency in the reasoning faculties, but almost a deficiency in instinctive discrimination". This was written of Englishmen; and it follows, from it, that even an Englishman, if idiomatic, must be well-nigh a compound of man and brute; the possession of "reasoning faculties" and that of "instinctive discrimination" being, respectively, the characteristics of the former and of the latter.

[1] "He requested Mrs. Unwin *would* invite them to tea." Southey, *Cowper's Works*, Vol. 1, p. 299.

[2] So far as the Index to Mr. White's book is serviceable, I omit paginal reference to the passages which I copy or discuss.

[3] Hear Mr. White further. "For the pronunciation *i-ther* and *ni-ther*, with the *i* long, which is sometimes heard, there is no authority, either of analogy or of the best speakers. It is an affectation, and, in this country, a copy of a second-rate British affectation. Persons of the best education and the highest social position in England generally say *eether* and *neether*."

On the contrary, the analogy of *eider, height,* and *sleight* favours the pronunciations *īther* and *nīther;* and so *either* and *neither* are, perhaps, most frequently sounded by cultivated Englishmen and Englishwomen. And in what sense are these pronunciations "a . British affectation"?

Their *a*, according to all the orthoepists that I know of, is exactly that in *an* and *at*. *Calf, half, rather*,[1] &c., have, indeed, like *father*, the Italian *a;* and yet I have heard persons of the highest culture, and not less in England than in America, pronounce these words with the flat sound of *a* in *pastor*. Provincialism is not necessarily vulgarity. If, manifested either in tone or in diction, it were the mortal sin which Mr. White appears to reckon it, his own perdition would be sealed irreversibly. The gossips that haunted his cradle must have been miserably underbred.

"Style, according to my observation, cannot be taught, and can hardly be acquired. Any person of moderate ability may, by study and practice, learn to use a language according to its grammar. But such a use of language, although necessary to a good style, has no more direct relation to it than her daily dinner has to the blush of a blooming beauty. Without dinner, no bloom; without grammar, no style. The same viand which one young woman, digesting it healthily and sleeping upon it soundly, is able to present to us again in but a very unattractive form, Gloriana, assimilating it not more perfectly in slumbers no sounder, transmutes into charms that make her a delight to the eyes of every beholder.[2] That proceeding is

---

In general, there is no ground for demur against Mr. B. H. Smart, as a recorder of English orthoepy. He should, however, have given *īther* and *ēther*, *nīther* and *nēther*. There are numerous words, too, in the *wh-* of which he sounds the *h*. One of his own pupils has expressed to me her amazement at his thus tilting against universal usage. In England, high and low alike, unless foreigners, or unless perverted by Mr. Smart and his followers, say *wat, weel, wence, wich, wim*, &c. &c. And this is the pronunciation which I learnt, as a lad, on the banks of the Connecticut, in Vermont. Irish and Scotch influence have pretty thoroughly obliterated it in America, I believe; but the fact of its prevalence among Vermonters as lately as in the days of my boyhood may prove that it dates back many generations, and that it may have crossed the Atlantic with our seventeenth-century ancestors.

"To this day," we are further informed, "*educated* clergymen, in reading the Bible, give the past participle its full, and not its contracted, form—*lov-ed*, not *lov'd*." P. 303.

Many an educated clergyman is, hereby, impliedly relegated to the ranks of the uneducated. Where did Mr. White procure the patent which authorizes him to say such things?

[1] Dr. Webster and Dr. Webster's editors pronounce *rather* to rime with *lather*. But who would go to them for orthoepy?

[2] The more rotund lady friends of the author must be cruelly ungrateful, if not alive to his appreciation of their good points. At p. 201, Gloriana seems to reappear,—"whom it was always a pleasure to look upon," with her "polished plumpness which so delighted my eye." In whatever sense "polished" is here to be taken, as applied to this adipose charmer, Mr.

Gloriana's physiological style. It is a gift to her. Such a gift is style in the use of language."

Just above, we have seen Mr. White in the character of elegantiæ arbiter. Here we have a practical sample of his notions of elegance; and I confidently put it to the reader, whether he does not find it rather of the grossest,—a good deal in the manner of Mr. Charles Reade. "I hope your dinner agreed with you?" was once asked by a person belonging to Mr. White's school of delicacy. "That is a matter which lies entirely between myself and my Maker" was the reply. It does not follow, because it is lawful to speak of Gloriana's ankles, or even of her legs, that it is becoming, unless we are utilizing the nymph in a treatise on dietetics, to go into particulars about the working of her chyle and chyme. For the rest, the thought of Gloriana has proved disastrous to Mr. White, from a syntactic point of view. Always impetuous, he loses the grammarian in the devotee, as he feels himself drawing nigh, in spirit, to this "blooming beauty". Her "blush" there is no discoverable pertinence in personifying; and yet it is personified, and femininized, and is declared to be out of direct relation to "her daily dinner".

"The authority of general usage", says Mr. White, at p. 24, "or even of the usage of great writers, is not absolute in language. There is a misuse of words which can be justified by no authority, however great, by no usage, however general." But the critic neglects to furnish us with any criterion, or set of criteria, his own mandates and ordi-

---

White's taste in womankind is, confessedly, somewhat à la Turque. But what was this to his readers?

In his work on Shakespeare, p. 240, Mr. White asserts, that "we do not hesitate to speak, if it be necessary to do so, of the stomach or bowels; but, in Elizabeth's time, the best-bred people designated those parts of the body by words the first of which is now heard only among boys, and the second never among decent people." When a writer expresses himself in this way, it is unavoidable to understand that he supposes himself to be stating what is true of his English-speaking contemporaries generally. The question of right and wrong has no place, as concerns the use of the terms on which Mr. White here remarks; but the fact is, that the freedom with which Americans talk of their stomachs and bowels is somewhat shocking to English notions of propriety. The two words which Mr. White only hints at have, also, different conventional values in America and in England. The first is, in England, far from being "now heard only among boys"; and, as to the other, there are occasions when it would there be accounted either squeamish or pedantic for "decent people" to cast about for a substitute.

nances excepted, by which to decide when the misuse of a word becomes impossible of justification. His animadversions, where original, are, I believe, in almost every case, founded either on caprice, on defective information, or on both; and, as he is in attack, so he often is in defence, even where he takes his stand on prescription. His dogmatism and positiveness are, at the same time, of that peremptory stamp which ensures the prompt submission of the unthinking multitude. We shall search in vain,—for all the world as if he had been bred at Oxford,—to find him conceding, as within the compass of the credible, the fallibility of his private judgments, or the inexhaustiveness of his meagre inductions.[1] Whatever he is not, he is always self-confident, and with the unflinching imperiousness of a Czar or a Pope. In 'tremble and believe' he epitomizes implicitly his one great precept; and, indeed, so infrequent are his deviations from this temper and tone, that to have forgone them would simply have evinced a nice sense of congruity.

If the constant flourishing, by Mr. White, of the censorial tomahawk and scalping-knife were to provoke some critic of congenial truculency to turn his favourite weapons upon him, he would have no title to complain. To fall into the clutches of such a Mohawk might, also, possibly be beneficial to him. But arrogant and ostentatious self-sufficiency, at least in philological questions, is best confronted, with a view to instruction, by a plain statement of facts ignorantly unrecognized and of analogies which superficial investigation has failed to discover; and Mr. White, for all his swaggering carriage, will be found, when viewed through the dry light of dispassionate truth, to be anything rather than redoubtable. This position, I am inclined to think, any intelligent and reflective reader of his strictures might make good by himself; but, as the bulk of mankind may be divided into the busy and the lazy, it has seemed worth while to submit a few specimens of those strictures to a little scrutiny.

---

[1] I would here remind those who possess *Words and Their Uses*, particularly of its eleventh chapter, *Is Being Done.* My critique on part of it was read before the American Philological Association in July, 1871, and was printed, in an imperfect form, in *Scribner's Monthly* for April last. The correct title of the paper, changed without my authority, is *On the Imperfect Tenses of the Passive Voice in English.*

"*Ize* and *ist*, two useful affixes for the expression of action and agency, are often ignorantly added when they are entirely superfluous, and when they are incongruous with the stem. They are Greek terminations, and cannot properly be added to Anglo-Saxon words. *Ist* is the substantive form; *ize*, the verbal. Among the monsters in this form, none is more frequently met with than *jeopardize*, a foolish and intolerable word, which has no rightful place in the language . . . . . It is formed by adding *ize* to a *verb* of long standing in the language, and which means 'to put in peril'; and *jeopardize*, if it means anything, means nothing more or less.

"*Experimentalize* is a word of the same character as the foregoing. It has no rightful place in the language, and is both uncouth and pretentious. The termination *ize* is not to be tacked indiscriminately to any word in the language, verbs and adverbs as well as adjectives and nouns, for the purpose of making new verbs that are not needed. It has a meaning; and that meaning seems to be continuity of action; certainly, action, and action which is not momentary. Thus, *equalize*, 'to make equal'; *naturalize*, 'to make as by natural' [*sic*]; *civilize*, 'to make civil'; so with *moralize*, *legalize*, *humanize*, etc. But the people who use *experimentalize* use it in the sense 'to try experiments'. *Experiment*, however, is both noun and verb, and will serve all purposes not better served by *try* and *trial*."

Mr. White should, rather, have begun with saying that our language exhibits, among words in *-ize* and *-ist*, but few of which the stem is not either Greek or Latin. By the law which he sets forth, *Americanize*, *Russianize*, *Mahometanize*, *Hinduize*, *Mormonize*, *Barnumize*, *galvanize*, *macadamize*, *nicotize*,[1] &c. &c., must, all, be cashiered; and so *alcalize*, *alcoholize*, *algebraize*, *heathenize*, with our old *dastardize*, *sluggardize*, and *wantonize*.[2] In the opinion of

---

[1] *Napoléoniser*, *Hausmanniser*, &c. show that the French coin personal verbs like ours in *-ize* as spontaneously as ourselves.

Professor Haldeman, in his *Affixes to English Words*, treats *analyse* as if it belonged to the class of verbs derived or imitated from those in -ιζω. *Analyse*—and so *paralyse*—is anomalous, and is out of place where he introduces it.

[2] De Foe uses the verb neuter *wizardize*. *A System of Magic*, &c. (ed. 1840), p. 216. Miss Carter, in her *Letters to Mrs. Montagu*, Vol. 1, p. 174, has the verb neuter *witticize*; and, if we dislike it, while we do not object to *witticism*, it is only because it is unfamiliar.

It seems very arbitrary that Mr. White, while condemning such words as *dastardize* and the rest, should in nowise reprehend — for, by implication, he does not reprehend—such words as *bastardize*, *bumperize*, *carrionize*, *galliardize*, *gluttonize*, *gormandize*, *miniardize*, *seigniorize*, *soberize*, *soldierize*, *sovereignize*, *villanize*, and *warrantize*; since who can ever have felt that they

Dr. Johnson, even *womanize*, though ."not used", is "proper". Exceptions, though they are ever so few, are not to be overlooked, when one propounds a law.

Jeopardize, however personally distasteful,[1] is not a thing to vex one's soul about, after the fashion of Mr. White, who, as we have seen, classes it among "monsters", styles it "foolish and intolerable", and rules that it "has no rightful place in the language". The origin of *jeopardize* which we find positively asserted is only speculative. And what if it really had grown out of another verb?[2] Are *appropriate, assassinate, conjecture, determine, fulminate,* and *repudiate,* if they were lengthened from *appropry, assassin, conject, determe, fulmine,* and *repudy,* "monstrous"? Are *cultivate, daunt, devastate, exemplify, extinguish, extirpate, impregnate, inundate, necessitate,* and *pulsate,* because we had, before their rise, the verbs *cultive, daw, devast, example, extinct, extirp, impregn, inunde, necessite,* and *pulse,* to be reckoned "foolish and intolerable"? Have *deaden, deafen, flatten, gladden, happen, lessen, madden, sharpen, shorten, straiten, strengthen* "no rightful place in the language", because they were preceded by the verbs *dead, deaf, flat, glad, hap, less, mad, sharp, short, strait, strength?* And are we to be denied a *fattened* capon, because our fathers feasted the prodigal son on a *fatted* calf? *Jeopardize*, quite as probably as not, set out, like *jeopard*,[3] from the substantive *jeopardy;* as *colonize, subsidize,* and *summarize* were based on *colony, subsidy,* and *summary.*[4] Again, it is an advantage to language, as precluding ambiguity, that a verb should have a termination suggestive of its being a verb; and *-ize* is such a termination.

---

were at all the more legitimate for not being crosses between Anglo-Saxon and Greek? I may add that I have met with all these words, in the course of my reading.

[1] Yet it is used by Southey, in *The Doctor* (monotome ed.), p. 32.

[2] Instead of *apostatize, characterize, christianize, emblematize, patronize, philosophize, scandalize, sermonize,* I have observed, in books written, it would seem, before they were devised, the verbs *apostate, character, christian, emblem, patron, philosophy, scandal, sermon.*

[3] *Jeopard* must have been preceded by *jeopardy*, anciently *jeupertye*, &c., *i. e., jeu parti.*

Like *jeopard* is Fuller's verb active *pillor*, from *pillory*. *Abel Redivivus* (1651), p. 436.

[4] To go to foreign languages, I might instance their verbs from which our *sympathize, theorize,* &c. were borrowed or imitated.

If we accede to Mr. White's view as to how we came by *jeopardize*, still the word has exact parallels in the candidate *martyrize*[1] and *proselytize*,[2] which, like it, may belong to the good English of the future, whether critics patronize them, ridicule them, or leave them alone.

The objections urged against *experimentalize* are the result of bad theorizing and want of discrimination, in pretty equal proportions. Mr. White's definition of *-ize* has been transcribed. Yet, how, until amended, it applies even to the verbs which he names,—*equalize*,[3] *naturalize*, *civilize*, *moralize*, *legalize*, and *humanize*,—it is hard to see. Here it is a particular modification of action, 'conversion', that seems to be implied by *-ize*. But there are other active verbs, as *anathematize*, *anatomize*, *baptize*, *satirize*, *terrorize*, of which the *-ize* must be explained differently; and so it must be in the neuter verbs *agonize*, *antagonize*, *apologize*, *attitudinize*, *botanize*, *criticize*, *dogmatize*, *geometrize*,[4] *philosophize*, *poetize*, &c. &c. In short, our verbs in *-ize*[5] are, to a large extent, of conventional import.[6] To come back

---

[1] As a verb active, it has been struggling into currency for centuries. Landor has used it as a verb neuter.

[2] Dr. Webster's editors mark *proselytize*, for 'convert', as "rare". To the authority, for it, of Burke may be added that of Dr. Arnold, &c.

Scrupulize, as a verb active and neuter, has been used for *scruple*. *Enthronize* was once preferred, by many writers, to *enthrone*. *Cantonize* is older than *canton*. And *favourize* has served as the equivalent of *favour*. "The queen mother of France . . . . praised Ramus, albeit he was known to *favourize* the Prince of Condé". Gabriell Harvey, *Pierce's Supererogation*, p. 110. Brathwait lengthens the verb active *hazard* into *hazardize*. *The English Gentleman*, &c., p. 297. Henry Earl of Monmouth uses *paragonize* for the verb active *paragon*. Still earlier, the same use of it occurs in the Scotch English of Lithgow. See *The Totall Discourse*, &c. (1632), p. 286.

[3] *Equalize* was long used where we use *equal*. Contrariwise, *equal* once had the sense now borne by *equalize*. "For there is not that vessell, in the world, that can measure men's tastes, nor that balance that can *equall* their likings, or give an even poyze to such uneven humours." *The Rogue, or, The Life of Guzman de Alfarache* (1623), Part 1, p. 24. See, for *equalize* = *equal*, Sir Arthur Gorges's Translation of Bacon's *De Sapientia Veterum*, p. 129; and Richard Fleckno's *A Relation*, &c., p. 165.

[4] Many a word like this might hastily be taken for an adaptation of a classical term. Γεωμετρέω, not γεωμετρίζω, is Greek. And there is no πολιτίζω, as original of Milton's *politize*. Also consider *mythologize*, *sympathize*, &c. &c.

[5] Some of the old ones were very lawless formations; for instance, *endenize*, Shakespeare's *infamonize*, Gabriell Harvey's *hypocrize*, and Dr. Donne's *critize*.

[6] *Signalize*, as used, in America, for *signal*, would, if the word were not preoccupied by another acceptation, be not only defensible, but preferable.

to *experimentalize*, why is it not as good as the verbs neuter *moralize, ruralize*, and *vocalize*, which, like it, are of adjectival origin? And what is there about it either "uncouth" or "pretentious"? But, what is most important of all, persons of intelligence who use it[1]—and a word is not to be impeached because the unintelligent misuse it,—do not make it a simple synonym of *experiment*. A boy may *experiment* in catching flies, or a smatterer may *experiment* in philology; but a philosopher, when he governs himself, in his investigations, by the complex of canons which constitute the experimental philosophy, *experimentalizes*.

"*Controversialist*, *conversationalist*, and *agriculturalist*, too frequently heard, are inadmissible, for reasons like to those given against *experimentalize*. The proper words are *controvertist*, *conversationist*, and *agriculturist*. The others have no proper place in the English vocabulary."

Far from concurring, as regards *controversialist*, in Mr. White's reprobation of it, we are to look upon the word as a felicitous instance, among accepted neoterisms, of the analogical superiority of a new formation to that which it has superseded. Many of our words in *-ist* we have borrowed; and others we have developed from substantival, adjectival, and other bases. The only verbs from which we have established their evolution are those in *-ize*. *Speculatist*, from *speculate*, never had any real root in usage; and it is fast following *controvertist* to oblivion.[2] As between

---

Its termination would at once distinguish it as a verb. The same may be said of *parodize*, in the thirty-first of Shenstone's *Letters;* and, if we had not already the verb *rival*, we should do well to frame *rivalize*, like the French *rivaliser*, unless we felt that we might need a verb to signify 'make a rival'.

[1] As Southey, Mr. J. S. Mill, Dr. Newman. Also see the references in Dr. Worcester's Dictionary.

[2] Both these words were favourites with Dr. Johnson. *Speculatist. Rambler*, Nos. 13, 14, 54, 77, 124, 126, 130, 156: *Idler*, Nos. 6, 19, 32. *Controvertist. Rambler*, Nos. 95, 106, 206: *Idler*, Nos. 19, 40, 91.

Dr. Johnson also adopted *computist;* he and Cowper use *rhymist;* Gabriell Harvey, *disciplinist;* Milton, *motionist* and *notist;* Glanvill, *drollist;* Samuel Richardson, *enquirist;* Burke and others, *schemist;* Southey, *libelist;* Charles Lamb, *petitionist;* Dean Milman and others, *contemplatist;* and Dr. Newman has *emanatist*. *Questionist* is purely collegiate. *Developist*, at this moment, is almost fashionable; and now and then one chances on *emancipist*, just such a portent as Goldsmith's *speculist*.

Conformist, *reformist*, and *separatist* came from abroad; and *copyist* is a modification of the old *copist*, from the French *copiste*.

speculatist and *controvertist*, the former, since its meaning is unequivocally suggested by *speculate* and *speculation*, is the less objectionable. That is *controverted* which is 'made matter of debate'; but *controvertist* reminds us directly of the verb, not of the past participle; and *controvert* is almost always used in the sense of 'oppugn' or 'deny'. *Controversialist* we connect immediately with *controversial* and *controversy*, which denote both defensive argumentation and offensive. In substitution for *controvertist*, we might, by starting with *controversy*, have made, from it, the harsh-sounding *controversist;* as we have *bigamist, diarist, prosodist,* and *rhapsodist*,[1] from *bigamy, diary, prosody,* and *rhapsody*. We recurred, however, in making the later word, to an adjective, for its base; and hence our *controversialist*,[2] in keeping with *literalist, loyalist, materialist, ministerialist, naturalist, rationalist, royalist*, &c. &c.[3] As for *conversationist* and *conversationalist, agriculturist* and *agriculturalist*,[4] as all are alike legitimate formations, it is for convention to decide which we are to prefer; as it has already decided, to take some very modern terms, in favour of *protectionist* and *secessionist*, but also in favour of *nationalist* and *specialist*.

As to mongrels, in like manner as Mr. White dooms, by wholesale, certain of them in *-ize*, he would deprive us of certain of them in *-ist*.

---

[1] *Rhapsodist* appears to be much older, in our language, than *rhapsodize*, which, however, is not so modern as the Dictionaries might lead one to suppose: it is used, as a verb active, by Sterne. See his *Works* (ed. 1819), Vol. 2, pp. 45, 128. Dr. Donne, in his *Biathanatos*, p. 32, has, instead of *rhapsodist, rhapsoder*.

[2] Archdeacon Todd quotes, under *controversialist*, Abp. Newcome, Warton, and Paley. I may add Jones, of Nayland, *Theological and Miscellaneous Works*, Vol. 1, pp. 341 (1769), 226; Vol. 5, p. 372: Cowper, *Works*, Vol. 15, p. 322: Southey, *Life of Wesley*, Vol. 2, pp. 206, 228: Lord Macaulay, *Essay on the Comic Dramatists of the Restoration*, and *Biography of Dr. Johnson:* and Dr. Newman, *Essay on the Miracles*, &c., pp. 75, 128, 154, 155; *Essays Critical and Historical*, Vol. 1, pp. 161, 165, 180, 183, 189, &c.

And who, in these days, Mr. White excepted,—for he scoffs at the word, as being of those which "have no proper place in the English vocabulary",—would ever hesitate to use it, and not *controvertist*?

Mr. White, by the way, is not original in his interdiction of *controversialist*. Under this word, in Dr. Webster's Dictionary (ed. 1848), we find: "The proper word is *controvertist*, which see." What right had Dr. Webster's editors to strike out this dictum?

[3] Southey has *commercialist;* Mr. J. S. Mill, *practicalist;* Mr. Ruskin, *proportionalist*.

[4] This form is used by Coleridge. See his *Church and State*, &c., p. 349.

"The ridiculous effect of the slang words *shootist*, *stabbist*, *walkist*, and the like, is produced by the incongruity of adding *ist* to verbs of Teutonic origin."

By this and other dicta, he would allow us neither *clubbist*, *harpist*, *red-tapist*, *timist*, nor *landscapist*.[1] Hybrids of this particular sort are not so much absolutely incongruous as rare. To the general class of which they are members, that is to say, the class of words in *-ist* not built up on Greek or Latin bases, belong *algebraist*, *Calvinist*, *druggist*, *feudist*, *galvanist*, *Jansenist*, *jargonist*,[2] *romanticist*, *Sanskritist*, and *tobacconist*;[3] and *journalist*, *larcenist*, *mannerist*, *routinist*, and *tourist* almost deserve to be placed in the same category. The freedom with which we attach *-ism* is illustrated by *cliqueism*, *Quakerism*, *toadyism*, and *truism*.

"*Er*, the Anglo-Saxon sign of the doer of a thing, is incorrectly affixed to such words as *photograph* and *telegraph*, which should give us *photographist* and *telegraphist*; as we say, correctly, *paragraphist*, not *paragrapher*; although the latter would have the support of such words as *geographer* and *biographer*, which are firmly fixed in the language."

In this we have one of the many evidences which Mr. White affords, that his views touching the development of our words are, in the highest degree, unscientific and anti-historical. *Photographer* and *telegrapher* he holds to be incorrect; similar to them, he says, is the hypothetical *paragrapher*; and this, he tells us, bad as it would be, would find support in *geographer* and *biographer*. But did *geographer* and *biographer* spring from *geograph* and *biograph*? The alleged parallelism is, then, without foundation. As I shall show, *photographer* and *telegrapher*, as English formatives, are far superior to *photographist* and *telegraphist*.

Many of our substantives in *-er*[4] are observable for their formation, and, in especial, those ultimately traceable to

---

[1] This accepted word is used by Mr. Ruskin, in *The Queen of the Air*, p. 199.

[2] Lord Macaulay uses it; but he by no means invented it.

[3] In the seventeenth century, the Scotchman Lithgow, imitating Englishmen his contemporaries, used this word for 'tobacco-smoker'. See *The Totall Discourse*, &c., p. 205.

[4] Where, by the by, did Mr. White learn that *-er* is "Anglo-Saxon"?

the Greek;[1] inasmuch as we have shaped them as if they were of any origin but Greek. For example, we have *astrologer, astronomer, bibliographer, biographer, chronologer, cosmographer, ethnographer, geographer, glossographer, hagiographer, historiographer, lexicographer, pantographer,*[2] *philologer, philosopher, theosopher, topographer,* &c. &c.; and the strikingly abnormal *geometer, idolater,* and *necromancer.*[3] In the case of these words, with a few exceptions, we seem to have operated directly on French forms in *-graphe, -logue, -nome, -sophe, -tre,* and *-cien.* Differently from most of the words particularized above, derivatives from verbs, no less than other derivatives, were felt to be desiderata, when occasion prompted recourse to the ideal τηλέγραφος[4] and φωτογράφος, as sources whence to enrich our vocabulary. *Photograph,* the substantive, very soon generated *photograph,* the verb, in analogy to *church, emblem, hymn, phrase, parody,* &c. &c. So far all is plain; and so is the generation of *photographic* and of *photography.*

To obtain an agential substantive complementing the verb *photograph,* the available processes are various. By recurring to φωτογράφος, and taking *geographer* for a model, we get *photographer.* Or *photographer* might be inferred from our verb *photograph;* as we have *cataloguer, chronicler, glosser,* from the verbs *catalogue,*[5] *chronicle, gloss.* Or it might be derived from the substantive *photograph;* as *epistler,*[6] *horoscoper,* and *stomacher* were evolved from *epistle, horoscope,* and *stomach.*[7] There are divers methods, likewise, by which *photographist* might be reached. A Greek would have seen, in φωτογραφιστής, a derivative of

---

[1] The originals of many of these words, it need scarcely be said, are, as verbal wholes, factitious.

[2] One is surprised to find so fastidious a classic as Gray using the corrupt form *pentagrapher. Correspondence of Gray and Mason,* p. 285. *Pentagraph* and *pentagraphic* are found in Sterne's *Tristram Shandy,* Vol. 1, ch. 23.

[3] From γεωμέτρης, εἰδωλολάτρης, and νεκρόμαντις, ultimately. With *necromancer* may be mentioned *chiromancer, geomancer,* &c. &c.

[4] If τῆλε and γράφω could be compounded, the agential substantive of τηλεγράφω would be τηλεγραφεύς, and there would be no premises for τηλέγραφος. Further, instead of τηλεγραφία, we should have τηλεγραφή. *Vide supra,* p. 42, note [5], and page 43, note [1].

[5] Long before it, we had the verb *catalogize.*

[6] This old word has lately been revived by English churchmen.

[7] Nash has *epitapher,* in his letter introductory to Greene's *Arcadia,* p. xviii. (in *Archaica,* Vol. 1); and *theamer,* for 'one who sets a theme', occurs in *Tarlton's Jests,* &c., p. 28.

φωτογραφίζω, a possible substitute for φωτογραφέω,[1] but called into existence, as such, very unnecessarily.[2] Among ourselves, *photographist*, as a natural outgrowth, from the substantive *photograph*, might, to mean 'dealer in photographs', have been suggested, inexactly, by *dialogist*,[3] *methodist*, *organist*, *physicist*, *psalmist*, connected with *dialogue*, *method*, *organ*, *physics*, *psalm*, but, like most words on the same type,—*essayist*[4] being an exception,—imported, ready-made, into our language.[5] Its accepted sense, 'one who photographs', is evidence, however, that it was taken from the verb *photograph;* and, though, among our vernacular formatives, a word in *-ist* is often found coupled with one in *-ize*,[6] we almost never form an agential by suffixing *-ist* to a verb.[7] *Photographist* and *telegraphist* are, consequently, hardly better than quite illegitimate.[8] Further, Mr. White, in the passage here

---

[1] Πολεμίζω, as sometimes equivalent to πολεμέω, is poetic. Regularly, φωτογραφίζω would mean 'act like a photograph, photographic machine, photographer', or the like.

[2] As to scores of our words in *-ist*, only by some such far-fetched deduction as this can they be wrested into obedience, even as regards form, to Greek analogies. The free and easy way in which we tack on the affix in question has been derived to us by the example of the French, Italian, and other peoples that have drawn their vocabularies from the classical languages. We have but few Greekish words in *-ist* so purely formed as *agonist*, *antagonist*, *catechist*, *exorcist*, *grammatist*, *panegyrist*, and *sophist*.

[3] Where did Dr. Webster's editors find, as real Greek and Latin words, their διαλογιστής and *dialogista ?*

[4] *Essayist*, though not from the Greek, I name for obvious reasons.

[5] On the supposition that *photography* antedated an agential of *photograph*, *photographist* might have been suggested by such words as *alchemist*, *geologist*, *philologist*, *strategist*,—allied to *alchemy*, *geology*, *philology*, *strategy*,—but could not have been devised, as an English formative, analogically; for here, again, we have naturalized exotics.

[6] As I have shown, at p. 37, the import of many of our verbs in *-ize* is wholly conventional. If, accordingly, we had taken the substantive *photograph*, and made from it *photographize*, *photographist* would have matched with it very naturally. Compare *botanize* and *botanist*. That *botanist* preceded *botanize* does not affect my argument. Now that we have *botanize*, *botanist* is, to us, 'one who botanizes'. So, *syllogist* would be 'one who syllogizes', 'syllogizer'.

[7] See p. 57, *supra*. *Dietist*, however derived, is hardly more English than *accompanist*, or than Miss Carter's *epistolist*. There remains *querist*, which, doubtless, set out from the verb *query*. Yet, to take it as a pattern on which to frame new substantives would be like taking *starvation*, *talkative*, *conducive*, and *nonsensical* as patterns for new substantives and adjectives.

[8] At p. 416, Mr. White writes: "If *engrave* (from *en* and *grapho*) gives us rightly *engraver* and *engraving*, *photograph* or *photograve* should give us *photographer* and *photographing*, and *telegraph*, *telegrapher* and *telegraphing*."

annotated, should also have set his stigma on *lithographer* and *stereotyper*, not to mention other kindred modernisms; for, by his rule, we ought to say *lithographist* and *stereotypist*.[1]

He prohibits us from annexing the affix *-er* to the verb *telegraph*, because, by the annexation, we produce a cross between Greek and English. Why not, then, reprobate *baptizer* and *sympathizer*? In all consistency, they are to be reprobated; and it passes ordinary understanding to perceive why he should endure *naturalize* and *civilize*, seeing that the Romans had no verbs in *-izo*.[2] Why, too, should he not lay an injunction on *alchemist*, *annalist*, *colourist*, *deist*, *druggist*, *duellist*, *linguist*, *mannerist*, *tobacconist*, *tourist*, *gormandizer*, *organizer*, *promoter*, *modernism*, *witticism*, and hundreds of other half-castes which have be-

Here Mr. White, by his *photograve*, prescribes, as a scientific procedure, a style of word-construction such as obtains restrictively during the period of a language when its imported accretions are moulded entirely by the popular will. As to the base of *engrave*, to take it directly from γράφω betokens much more of boldness than of prudence. The cognate words in Gothic and Anglo-Saxon had, incontrovertibly, the same ancestor with γράφω: but *grave* belongs to the oldest English; and, hence, there is no likelihood that we are to trace it from the Greek. Nor is it at all probable that we have to go further than to France for the preposition exhibited in such words as *engrave*, *ensphere*, and *enthrone*. At the time Mr. White wrote as above, *photographer* and *telegrapher* had not yet seemed to him objectionable, as being mongrels; and, in his work on Shakespeare, *palæographists* occurs at p. 95, and *palæographers*, at p. 108. At present, it is hard to see why he should abide *engraver*, instead of *engravist*, or, rather, *engraphist*.

When Mr. White expressed himself as in the passage quoted at the beginning of this note, there is a violent presumption that he had much to be told touching the antiquity of the verb *grave*. Still, he puts off a critic, in reward for pointing out to him that the word is in Chaucer, by saying that this, "to a man who, having read Chaucer, for pleasure, from his boyhood, has, within the last six months, reread every word of him, and of Gower, carefully and critically, is valuable, nay, invaluable, information." P. 423. We have seen, in the case of *experience*, how far his memory serves him to recall what he must constantly have been happening on all his life; and could vanity itself suppose that the pretence of knowledge herein implied would not be perfectly transparent to everybody?

As an argument that our *engrave* got its preposition from the Greek, Mr. White tells us: "the English-formed participle *engraven* I do not know in literature three hundred and fifty years old." P. 424. In Elyot's *Governour* (1531), p. 92, I find *ingrave*; and the verb *engraver*, in one sense, is, as Raynouard proves, very old French. Will Mr. White still be "inclined to the opinion, not only that *grave* is a direct descendant, as it is a perfect counterpart, of γράφω, but that the appearance of *engrave* in English is a consequence of an acquaintance with the Greek compound ἐγγράφω"?

[1] The French word is *stéréotypeur*.

[2] They had verbs in *-isso*; but they were very few.

come lexical fixtures? The answer is, that there are very many words in our language, to ascertain the analogical soundness of which, it is necessary to visit regions undreamt of in the philosophy of Mr. White; that, as a philologist, he has no principles deserving to be called scientific; and that, therefore, his premises involve the most monstrous conclusions.

Presidential being a word which it falls to the lot of Mr. White to read or hear almost daily, we may judge, from his critique on it, how the burthen which we bear, in common, through this vale of tears must be aggravated to him by the fancied abomination.

"This adjective, which is used among us now more frequently than any other not vituperative, laudatory, or boastful, is not a legitimate word. Carelessness or ignorance has saddled it with an *i*, which is on the wrong horse. It belongs to a sort of adjectives which are formed from substantives by the addition of *al*. For example, *incident, incidental; orient, oriental; regiment, regimental; experiment, experimental*. . . . The proper form is *presidental*, as that of the adjectives formed upon *tangent* and *exponent* is *tangental* and *exponental*. *Presidential, tangential*, and *exponential* are a trinity of monsters which, although they have not been lovely in their lives, should yet in their death be not divided. . . . . Euphony, no less than analogy, cries out for the correct forms, *presidental, tangental*, and *exponental*."

Whoever invented *presidential*, Dr. Peter Heylin[1] used it in the first year of Charles I. Whether its originator had the vernacular word *presidence* or *presidency* to serve for its base, it is needless to investigate. *Præsidentia*, factitious, but yet strictly analogical, taken along with the existence of *president*, was quite ground enough to supply it with a raison d'être. Covering an abstract, it would

---

[1] "This institution of these *Presidentiall* Courts was, at first, a very profitable ordinance, and much eased the people." *A Full Relation of Two Journeys*, &c. (1656), p. 134.

The part of this book from which the clause adduced is taken was written in 1625. Heylin intends to represent "siéges *présidiaux*", or "curiae *præsidiales*", the judges of which were called "juges *présidiaux*". At p. 292, Heylin has "Courts *Presidiall*".

Archdeacon Todd's earliest authority for *presidential* is Glanvill. Besides the passage quoted from him, by the Archdeacon, I find the following, of prior date, in his *Essays*, &c. (1676), VI., p. 26: "Thus Origen and others understand that to be spoken by the *presidential* angels." In qualifying 'angels', *presidential* has reference to *presidency*, much rather than to *president*.

also cover the concrete corresponding to that abstract. Just so, *judicial* is equally suggestive of *judgment* and of *judge; ministerial* refers alike to *minister* and to *ministry;* and *penitential* tears must be those of a *penitent,* while they are those of *penitence.*[1] *Præsidens* would regularly give birth to *præsidentia;* and their adjective would be *præsidentialis.*[2] Our *presidential* is complementary to both *president* and *presidency;* and *presidental*[3] would be complementary to *president* only: but we required an adjective complementary to both that and *presidency;* and we have it in *presidential.* *Tangential*[4] and *exponential,*[5] to denote equally pro-

---

[1] Conventionally, we limit the reference of *deferential, expediential, influential,* and *presential* to *deference,* &c., only.

[2] From *adolescens* was evolved *adolescentia;* and their adjective might have been *adolescentialis;* as *substantialis* was the adjective of *substans* and *substantia.*

Fuller uses *accidential,* as if he assumed the existence of *accidentialis* and *accidentia.* "The substantiall use of them might remain, when their *accidential* abuse was removed." *The Appeal of Injured Innocence,* &c. (1659), Part 1, p. 69.

[3] Both *présidental* and *présidentiel* are recognized, by M. Littré, as good French. Richelet (1732) knows only the first.

[4] It is used by Addison, *Tatler,* No. 43. Our old word for *tangent* was *touch-line.*

[5] "These words and *presidential,*" says Mr. White, "are the only examples of their kind which have received the recognition, and have been stamped with the authority, even of dictionary-makers." Sweeping statements of this sort are not over-safe. Some of the dictionaries enter *precedential,*—on Mr. White's reasoning, from *precedent,* the substantive,—vouching Thomas Fuller for it; and Fuller has used the word again and again. "Wherefore all their actions in that time are not *precedential* to warrant posterity." *The Appeal,* &c., Part 1, p. 41. Also see Part 3, p. 8; and *Mixt Contemplations in Better Times,* xvi. Brathwait has, instead, *precedental.* *A Boulster-lecture,* p. 272: *The English Gentleman,* &c., p. 435: *The Turtle's Triumph* (1641), p. 8. Further, to Mr. White, *consequential* ought to be from the substantive *consequent,* which we had before *consequence.*

Tangentiel and *exponentiel* are, both, French. The latter dissatisfied Condillac; but it satisfies M. Littré. And why? It comes, he says, from *exponens,* as *potentiel* comes from *potens!* This is almost as bad as Mr. White's derivation of *presidential.*

Our ancestors once used *concurrent, contingent, exigent, inconvenient, occurrent,* and *sequent,* where we use *concurrence,* &c. *Precedent,* the substantive, —often carelessly spelled *president,*—from the imaginary *præcedentia,* was allowed to remain unchanged, to avoid the duality of meaning, 'example' and 'priority', which would, otherwise, have devolved on *precedence.*

Accidence, the grammatical term, is a corruption of *accidents.* Like plurals are not uncommon in oldish authors. Sir Thomas Elyot, in his *Governour,* fol. 8, 66, has *inhabitance* and *experience,* for *inhabitants* and *experients;* Robert Southwell, in his *Triumphs over Death,* p. 17, has *accidence,* for the ordinary *accidents;* Brathwait, in *The English Gentleman,* &c., p. 388, has *ingredience,* for *ingredients.* Differently, Brathwait, in *The Turtle's*

perties and things, are, in like manner, defensible. Of the same class with them is *agential,* a word of prime utility, as referring, indifferently, to *agent* and to *agency.* As regards the sound of the words here treated of, a private monitress entertained by Mr. White, and whom he is pleased to call "Euphony", "cries out", we are informed, for *presidental, tangental,* and *exponental.* The news of this eccentric clamour may be interesting to the curious; but the lady, it may be suspected, is wailing a solo; and the new voice of one crying in the wilderness is not likely to work conversion beyond the sphere of its present very select audience. Is *influential,* or *providential,* or *reverential* dissonant?

Condescending to instruct us about some of our commonest verbs, Mr. White prescribes, as exclusively being correct, the preterites *brake, spake, gat, bide,* and the participles *drunken, sitten,* and *bidden.* To say "has *sat*" is called an error corresponding to "he *done* it". "Many persons abbreviate *gotten* into *got*". Also:

"*Snew* is the regular preterite of *snow,* the regular past participle of which is not *snowed,* but *snown.* . . . . *Snow, snowed, snowed* is as irregular as *throw, throwed, throwed* would be, or *blow, blowed, blowed.*[1] . . . . . In some parts of New England, and notably in Boston, we still hear, from intelligent and not uneducated people, 'he *shew* (pronounced *shoo*) me the way', which is sneered at by persons who do not know that *shew* is the regular, and *showed* an irregular, preterite, the use of which is justified only by custom."

Charles James Fox speaks of our ancestors' having, on a certain point, "fairly gained a conquest over the natural enemy of writers, which I consider strict grammar to be".[2] A remark more absurd than this has seldom been com-

---

Triumph, p. 23, uses *equivalence* for *equivalent;* and, like many of his predecessors, Henry Earl of Monmouth, in his *Advertisements from Parnassus,* p. 168, uses *ingrediences,* for *ingredients.*

Some of the peculiarities noted in the last paragraph are due, perhaps, to the old printers.

[1] Can Mr. White require to be informed that *throwed* and *blowed,* for *threw* and *blew,* occur in many a good old author? But who uses *snew?*

[2] *Works of Samuel Parr,* Vol. 1, p. 615. Swift, in his *Proposal for Correcting, Improving, and Ascertaining the English Tongue,* says, with like absurdity, of our language, that, "in many instances, it offends against every part of grammar".

mitted to paper. Any "strict grammar" for which a basis is claimed apart from usage must be a species of theology, of which prophets by divine designation alone possess the key. That awful fetish, "general and abstracted grammar", which Fox names with bated breath, and yet recreantly ejects from his pantheon, turns out, indeed, on scrutiny, to be particular and altogether distracted nonsense. The materials which it undertakes to manipulate are, in large measure, so many independent and irrelate atoms; and these it attempts to work into a system imported from cloudland. Exceptions, so called,—which analogize with special providences in the mundane order,—have a place assigned to them. But some of the atoms aforesaid resolutely refuse to fit in where they ought, and will be square, though they ought to be round; and then—so much the worse for them. "General and abstracted grammar" has, however, been definitively exploded by rational philology. What this consists of we have dissertations and manuals, by the shelfful, to inform us. But, to these, *Words and Their Uses* bears the same relation that alchemy bears to chemistry.

Not wholly by way of digression, let us pause, for a moment or two longer, to examine Mr. White's incoherent fiction as to the occasional lunatic performance, idle pugnacity, and eventual overthrow of his bugbear, grammar.

> "Speech, the product of reason, tends more and more to conform itself to reason; and, when grammar, which is the formulation of usage, is opposed to reason, there arises, sooner or later, a conflict between logic, or the law of reason, and grammar, the law of precedent, in which the former is always victorious."[1]

Now, by usage of speech we mean the forms of it which are customarily employed; and, by grammar and lexicography, orderly records thereof. Although, then, speech tended "more and more to conform itself to reason," grammar could never be opposed to reason; since, as speech changes, itself changes.[2] We are told, however, that, now and then, it

[1] P. 23.

[2] Every assemblage of absurdities must have its climax; and Mr. White climaxes his in his tenth chapter, *The Grammarless Tongue*,—English, to-wit.
Most confused notions of the province of grammar are very common. Dean Alford remarks, on the phrase "a *mean* to an end": "This is not English, though it may be correct in grammatical construction." *A Plea for the Queen's English*, p. 29.

actually does come to be so opposed; and it is the grammarians that are responsible for the opposition.[1] Speech, by this account of it, must be, forsooth, a most froward style of entity. "The product of reason", while left to itself, behaves rationally enough; but, once let a grammarian get hold of it, and there is no saying that it will not go disloyal and demented out of hand. Whenever this befalls, reason takes immediate steps for its coercion and recovery; and grammar, in the end, resipiscent and sane as of old, goes forth properly clothed and in its right mind. To borrow the terminology of the Rev. Philocalvin MacFrybabe, a sort of indefectible grace thus saves it from the fate of an utter castaway.

Why the grammarians should be prone to encourage rebellion against reason is a mystery on which we are offered no light; and, possibly, it is not worth exploring. But let us not be ungrateful for the tuition which releases us from everything like servile dependence on such dangerous guides. 'Are you a grammarian, good sir?' 'No.' 'Then it may be credited that you are exempt from a fatal aptitude to wrongheadedness, and that you may have direct commerce with reason.' This presumption, it must be confessed, is comforting, as far as it goes; only it is not given to every one to enjoy those intimate relations with reason which have been vouchsafed to Mr. White, as one of the elect. In this we have, with all clearness, the doctrine of the philological higher law and inner light,—enthroned aloft, beside King Sigismund, supra grammaticam. Identify it as one may with reason, it differs in nowise from Fox's "general and abstracted grammar", a something paramount to usage.

Dismissing mythology, let us now contemplate sober realities. That which, in contradistinction to the language

---

By "English", nothing can be meant, here, but the English usage of the present day; for we all know that the time was when "a *mean*" was as rife as 'a *means*', if not more so. Let a thing be "correct in grammatical construction", and yet "not English", and it follows that grammar is a fixed something, to which usage may conform, or may not, as it happens. The Dean, in the present instance, would not be thought to condemn the "grammatical construction" which he speaks of. What then? Grammar and usage are, both, good things, in their way; but it is not at all requisite that they should harmonize. This is marvellously like popular theology.

[1] "Grammarians . . . devote themselves to formulating that which use has already established." P. 338.

of the brute creation, we call speech is, unquestionably, a product of reason. But the products of reason are uniform, or multiform, according to the subject-matter submitted to its operation. Where number and quantity are concerned, the results at which reason arrives are uniform. But very different, as data and results, are, respectively, the original materials of speech and that which reason shapes out of those materials. The cast of a die is absolutely impossible of prediction; and yet we know that it obeys the laws of motion: and perhaps the only fact that can be posited as fundamental, in accounting for the origin and the mutation of speech, is, that reason is determined, in its choice of sounds answering to given conceptions, by subtile properties, in the subject-matter acted upon, which are perpetually varying. And hence it is, that perpetual variation is a characteristic of speech. Instead, however, of asserting change to be a law of speech, Mr. White asserts that speech "tends more and more to conform itself to reason"; a singular procedure for that which is "the product of reason", and one which we should rather expect from a product of unreason brought under rationalizing influences. Speech, cultivated, ameliorates; uncultivated, or miscultivated, it deteriorates. But, on Mr. White's principles, it is constantly improving, and, provided it were freed from the shackles of grammar, would improve the faster; the ascertainment of usage operating to distort its rational conformation and to impede its natural development. The Latin of the iron age should, therefore, be called Latin of the golden age; and Cicero, by the side of Jornandes, is a fumbling barbarian. The language in which Noah, when he had cast off his hawser, tried to hearten his friends left out in the wet, was the most inefficient of jargons, in comparison with the clicking of a Hottentot; and, about by doomsday, we shall attain to a rationality of expression no less unimaginable now than it will be unneeded then. The case standing thus, how it is that Mr. White wishes to revive English which has become obsolete, and how it is that he is so sorely grieved by the English of his contemporaries, may well perplex us. And this brings us to his antique preterites and past participles.

What if *brake, gat, snew,* and *sitten* were accepted English[1] once? The fact is of interest, certainly, from a philological point of view; but there is an end. If they came down from Heaven, let us, by all means, reinstate them with all possible speed. Unless convinced of their celestial derivation, our ancestors who used them, if they had denounced as wrong any forms but their Gothic or Anglo-Saxon originals, would have done precisely as Mr. White does. But he is not so hard a master as, at the first blush, he looks to be. He discriminates, in tenderness to us benighted moderns; and it behoves us to be thankful for small mercies. "*Got* having, by custom, been poorly substituted for *gat*, . . we may say 'He *got* away', instead of 'He *gat* away'." It is a relief to be told so. Again:

> "But, *got* being the preterite of *get*, as *did* is of do, 'He had *got*' is an error of the same class as 'He had *did*'; and, on the other hand, if *got* is the past participle of *get*, as *done* is of *do*, 'He *got*' is really no worse than 'He *done*',—only more common among people of some education."

The "we" and "the people of some education" are the same persons; and Mr. White so expresses himself as to be included among these abjects. Duly humbled by a sense of our educational deficiencies, and grateful, withal, for the consideration shown to them, let us stick, then, to our preterite *got*. The participles *gotten* and *sitten*, as belonging to the speech of transcendental grammarians and the gods, the vulgar may be permitted to honour from afar. *Shew*, for *showed*, it is melancholy to see that Mr. White is deterred, by want of proper courage, from extending his ægis over. *Showed*, as against *shew*,[2] "is justified only by custom". The same justification, and no

---

[1] I doubt much whether *shew*, for the preterite *showed*, ever was so. I have seen it but once in any English book not provincial,—the translation of *Il Cardinalismo di Santa Chiesa* (1670), p. 326. As a Scotticism, it is common enough, alike in old books and in recent. See my second edition of William Lauder's *Ane Compendious and Breve Tractate*, p. 23; note on line 7.

[2] I write in a part of England where the vulgar invariably use *shew* for the preterite *showed*, &c. &c. "This morning, before the *dag* was off, I *sew* seed *enow* for this week, and then *wed* two beds", was the reply returned to me by my gardener, a few days ago. In the dialect of the same sturdy conservative, a hare caught in a wire-fence "*shruck* terrible"; and *wenchen* is, to him, as natural a plural as *oxen*. Provincialisms, which are, in the main, remnants of antiquity, are objects of curiosity; and there they may be left.

other, is all that can be challenged for *clung, crept, helped, hung, might,* and a thousand more words, instead of the *clang, crope, holpe, hing, moughte,* &c., of two or three centuries ago. Why, in the case of these words, are not the ancient forms pronounced to be the only true ones? Why half measures, or measures of any other fraction? Why mount a cod-piece, but decline trunk-hose and a pig-tail?

The word *bountiful*, according to Mr. White,

> "is very generally misused both in speech and in writing. The phrase 'a *bountiful* dinner', 'a *bountiful* breakfast', or, to be fine, 'a *bountiful* repast', is continually met with in newspapers. . . . *Bountiful* applies to persons, not to things,[1] and has no reference to quantity."

Long ago, it may be presumed, the reader has discovered, in Mr. White, the peculiarity, that, when he employs language which, with ordinary people, indicates the communication of facts, he is only announcing his own opinions of what should be facts; and it is rare indeed that these are not officious idiosyncrasies. *Munificus*, literally, 'gift-making', qualified both the giver and his gift; and our *munificent* is applied with equal extension. So, too, *liberalis* was, and *liberal* now is; and *healthful* means both 'free from sickness' and 'salubrious'. Also consider *lavish, prodigal, profuse,* &c. &c. *Bountiful*, similarly, is, in good usage, applied alike to persons and to things.[2] That the dictionaries have overlooked the use of this word which Mr. White exostracizes goes for nothing. That use has the sanction of the *Prayer-Book*,[3] of Steele,[4]

---

[1] When a thing is personified, it may, of course, be qualified by *bountiful*, in its subjective acceptation. Mr. White forgets this. "*Bountiful hands*". Sir Arthur Gorges, Translation of Bacon's *De Sapientia Veterum* (1619), p. 131: Fuller, *Abel Redevivus*, p. 435. "*Bountiful hand*". Brathwait, *The English Gentleman*, &c., p. 89: De Foe, *A System of Magic*, p. 336. More such instances are given further on.

[2] Even Dr. Johnson's second definition of *bountifully*, the perfectly unobjectionable expression "in a *bountiful* manner", should have kept Mr. White from saying that the adjective "applies to persons, not to things".

[3] "Thy *bountiful* grace and mercy". Collect for the Fourth Sunday in Advent. In II. Cor., 9, 6, *bountifully* is opposed to *sparingly*.

[4] "Voice, stature, motion, and other gifts must be very *bountifully* bestowed by nature; or labour and industry will but push the unhappy endeavourer in that way the further off his wishes." *Tatler*, No. 167.

Lady Bradshaigh wrote, in 1750: "I want only power to send you a present which I would allow you to call *bountiful*." *Correspondence of Samuel Richardson*, Vol. 6, p. 56.

Johnson,[1] Henry Brooke,[2] Burke,[3] Southey,[4] and Mr. De Quincey,[5] and, not improbably, is nearly as old as the word itself.[6]

---

1 "Others on whom the blessings of life are more *bountifully* bestowed." *Rambler*, No. 186.

"He seems to have been well acquainted with his own genius, and to know what it was that nature had bestowed upon him more *bountifully* than upon others." *Life of Milton.*

2 "Nurse went up-stairs with a most *bountiful* cut of home-baked bread and butter." *Fool of Quality*, Vol. 1, p. 167.

3 "The late *bountiful* grant from His Majesty's ministers." *Speech on the Nabob of Arcot's Debts.*

"To make this *bountiful* communication", &c. *Reflections on the Revolution in France.*

4 "As those distinctions have been more shaded into each other, has there not been less *bountiful* patronage on the one side, and less of the kindly and grateful feeling of dependence on the other?" *Colloquies*, Vol. 2, p. 45.

5 "From the beginning, it presumed a most *bountiful* endowment of heroic qualifications." *Works*, Vol. 14, p. 435.

"This *bountiful* provision of nature." *Logic of Political Economy* (ed. 1844), p. 137.

Bounteous goes with *bountiful;* and Dr. Johnson—*Rambler*, No. 181—has "*bounteous* allotment". A like use of the word is common in hymns with which all of us are familiar. *Bounteous* qualifies "rewards", "liberality", &c., in Sir Thomas Elyot's *Governour* (1531), fol. 39, 114, 173, 195 (ed. 1580). In fol. 67, *bounteously* means 'copiously'. "*Bounteous* graces". Gabriell Harvey, *Pierce's Supererogation* (1593), p. 62 (in *Archaica*, Vol. 2). "*Bounteous* goodness", "*bounteous* liberality". Dr. Donne, *Polydoron* (1631), pp. 57, 78, 131.

6 Instances earlier than the oldest of those which follow no doubt exist.

"Those principles be these and such lyke. That the soule is immortal, and, by the *bountiful* goodnes of God, ordeined to felicitie." Raphe Robynson, Translation of Sir Thomas More's *Utopia* (1556), p. 106 (ed. 1869).

"By his *bountifull* liberalitie, professors of dyvers tongues were instituted and appointed." *Pasquine in a Traunce*, fol. 112.

"A large and *bountifull* intrest". Barnabe Riche, *Farewell to Militarie Profession*, p. 183. "To reward liberally, to give *bountifully*". *Id.*, *ibid.*, p. 75.

"These . . . Signior Bartolo . accepted . with great gratfulness, that so good and *bountiful* a gift merited". *Tarlton's Jests*, &c., p. 78.

"Did I not intend to deal a *bountiful* alms of courtesy, who, in my case, would give ear to the law of oblivion, that hath the law of talion in his hands?" Gabriell Harvey, *A New Letter*, &c. (1593), p. 14 (in *Archaica*, Vol. 2).

"Free and *bountiful* hospitality." Verstegan, *Restitution of Decayed Intelligence*, &c. (1605), p. 55 (ed. 1673).

"*Bountiful* blessings", "*bountiful* entertainment", "*bountiful* reflection", "*bountiful* favour". John Taylor, the water-poet, *Works* (ed. 1630), Vol. 1, pp. 119, 137; Vol. 2, p. 101; Vol. 3, p. 77.

"Which proceeded not from that the scituation of Rome was more *bountifull* then theirs, but onely from the different course they tooke." Edward Dacres, Translation of *Machiavel's Discourses* (1636), p. 273.

"*Bountiful* disposition", "*bountiful* legacies". Brathwait, *The English Gentleman*, &c., pp. 36, 241.

"And here I may seasonably appeal unto the apprehensions of men, ...

"*Convene* is much perverted from its true meaning by many people who cannot be called illiterate. Thus: 'The President *convened* Congress'. *Convene* (from *con* and *venio*) means 'to come together'. The right word, in this case, is *convoke*, which (from *con* and *voco*) means 'to call together'. The President *convokes* Congress in special session, and then Congress *convenes*. *Convene* is misused in the Constitution of the United States itself, which is singularly free from errors in the use of language."

That the use here condemned was ever before considered as faulty, or will ever again be drawn into question, is scarcely supposable. Not to go into antiquity,[1] writers such as Dr. Johnson,[2] Cowper,[3] Southey,[4] Coleridge,[5] Lord Macaulay,[6] Abp. Manning,[7] and Dr. Newman,[8] make *convene* a verb active; it differs from *convoke*,

---

why the free will of Atove or Ahad should be lesse *bountifull* then the minds of well-meaning men", &c. Henry More, *Philosophicall Poems* (ed. 1647), pp. 411, 412.

"Those hands . . . are now ever open for alms-deeds and *bountiful* distribution to the needy." *Id.*, *Mystery of Godliness*, p. 513.

"*Bountiful* maintenance", "*bountiful* contributions". Fuller, *The Holy State and the Profane State*, pp. 86, 267. Also see Fuller's *Mixt Contemplations in Better Times*, XIX.

The following phrases are from *Abel Redevivus*. "*Bountiful* hospitality": Dr. Featly, pp. 307, 550. "*Bountiful* charity": Dr. Isaacson, page unnumbered. "*Bountiful* manner": Anon., p. 515.

"Whereupon Almighty God not onely declares his acceptance of that pious resolution, but rewards it with a *bountifull* promise." Barrow, *Works*, Vol. 1, p. 162.

"This if they cannot do with a quiet mind, they are left free, by the Church, to enjoy a laical indulgence, which is very large and exceeding *bountiful*." Puller, *Moderation*, &c., p. 76.

[1] Dr. Johnson quotes Clarendon and Pope. Also see *Eikon Basilike*, Ch. 1, 4, 20; Hobbes, *Works*, Vol. 2, p. 91; Pearson, *An Exposition of the Creed*, p. 466; Sanderson, *Sermons*, Vol. 1, Preface, § 4; and Jeremy Collier, *Essays upon Several Moral Subjects*, Part III. (ed. 1705), p. 130. To the names in the text I may add those of Horace Walpole, Edward Moore, and Lord Chesterfield. See the *World*, Nos. 160, 182, 197.

Convene was preceded by *convent*, most generally a verb active, in the sense of 'summon'. No doubt *convent* is older than Bishop Bale, who used it before 1563. See his *Kynge Johan* (ed. 1838), p. 36. Also see Brathwait's *English Gentleman*, &c., p. 200; Gataker and Fuller, in *Abel Redevivus*, pp. 198, 200 201, 211, 378; and Heylin, *Examen Historicum* (1659), Part 1, pp. 71, 147.

[2] *Rambler*, No. 91. [3] *Works*, Vol. 1, p. 180.

[4] *Espriella's Letters*, Vol. 2, p. 10. [5] *Church and State*, &c., p. 334.

[6] In his *Essays on Hallam's Constitutional History and on Warren Hastings*.

[7] *The Unity of the Church*, p. 129.

[8] *Essay on the Miracles*, &c., pp. 6, 201: *Essays Critical and Historical*, Vol. 2, p. 320.

as 'cause to come together' differs from 'call together'; and, from the competition of *assemble* and *meet,* the verb neuter *convene,* which never was very common, is, at least in England, rapidly obsolescent. If, for a reason like that alleged, "to *convene* Congress" be incorrect, then, since *florescere, resistere,* and *revivere* have none but neuter senses,[1] and *partiri, revolvere,* and *separare,* none but active senses, it is bad English to speak of '*flourishing* a sword', '*resisting* evil', and '*reviving* dormant feelings', or to say 'he has *parted with* his common sense', 'the earth *revolves round* the sun', and 'the friends *separated*'. Mr. White really does not seem aware that his own good pleasure is insufficient to brand as wrong that which everybody else thinks to be right.

Though he admits that *divine,* in the sense of "clergyman", "is supported by long usage and high authority",[2] Mr. White declares that "This use of this adjective as a noun has a parallel in the calling *philosopher* 'a philosophic', which is done in a newspaper-article before me." There is not only all the difference, here, between what is established and what is not, but more. By a *divine* we do not mean 'a divine person';[3] but we should mean, by a

It is deplorable how far Mr. White is unacquainted with good usage. At p. 418, he calls *risible* "the counterpart" of *laughable.* Yet *risible,* save as signifying "able to laugh", &c., *risibilis,* has never been accepted English, notwithstanding Dr. Johnson's "*risible* scenes in the farce of life", "*risible* absurdities", and "*risible* part" of a play. Scotch may not be called into court; and so Mr. White, on his ground for scouting *proven,* is bound to admit. At p. 422, shifting his position, he tells us: "*Risibilis* (which, I have heard it whispered, is not the best Latin) is, of course, the counterpart of *risible,* or was when I went to school." *Risible* had, then, when Mr. White went to school, a certain meaning; and that meaning he recollected, on being reminded that it was not 'laughable'. He refuses to acknowledge his error, and would have us believe that all such little matters have been perfectly well known to him from his boyhood. Whatever philological learning he possesses is, on the contrary, in all seeming, the latest of opsimathies.

[1] The verb active *resurrect* I cannot admire; and yet it is perfectly legitimate, for all that Mr. White objects to it. He calls it "this amazing formation". Quite as much so is *correct, erect,* or *select,* as a verb: for the change from neuter into active, or the reverse, is a trifle, as we see above. Southey uses *resurrectionize;* and it is better than *resurrect,* since *resurrectionist* is fully established. Richard Franck, in his *Northern Memoirs,* p. 202, uses *insurrect* of 'vapours'.

[2] Mr. White here employs both *divine* and *clergyman* in senses now uncurrent in England.

[3] *Divine,* the adjective, and *divinely* have been used with reference to the science of divinity and its professors. Dr. Peter Heylin writes of "philo-

philosophic, 'a philosophic person'; and, if we had adopted the word in that sense, we should have done as we have done by *ascetic, dyspeptic, ecclesiastic, itinerant, lunatic, mendicant, mimic, mortal, official, paralytic, resident*. Dr. Donne,[1] quite analogically, employed, as personal substantives, *panegyric* and *satiric*; Heylin,[2] *academical*; Fuller[3] and others, *chymic* and *fantastic*; Hobbes,[4] *democratical;* and De Foe,[5] *enthusiastic. Obituary*, for 'obituary notice', and *monthly*, for 'monthly publication', are, in Mr. White's estimation, "equally at variance with reason and with good taste."[6] Then it is unreasonable and vulgar to call babies *innocents*, to term grown-up persons *adults*, to talk of *ancients* and *moderns*, *juniors* and *seniors*, *annuals* and *perennials*, and, in short, to employ as a substantive any word that was, originally, an adjective or a participle.[7] Scores of substantivized adjectives which were

---

sophical, civil, or *divine* discourses". *Examen Historicum* Part 2, p. 33. Again, in Part 1, Introduction, § 9: "But he that looks upon His Majesties last Paper will finde that he had learnedly and *divinely* refel'd all their arguments." Also see the full title of Feltham's *Resolves*.

[1] *Biathanatos* (no date), pp. 143, 43. [2] *A Full Relation*, &c., p. 82.

[3] "True it is, he was very wild in his youth, till God,—the best *Chymic*, who can fix quicksilver itself,—graciously reclaimed him." *The Holy State and the Profane State*, p. 80.

"Not like our *fantastics*, who, having a fine watch, take all occasions to draw it out to be seen." *Ibid.*, p. 245.

For other instances, older and later, of the substantive *fantastic*, once a very common word, see Brathwait, *The English Gentleman*, &c., p. 390; Glanvill, *Essays*, &c., VII., p. 24; Henry More, *Annotations upon Lux Orientalis*, &c. (1682-3), p. 257.

[4] *Works*, Vol. 6, pp. 199, 200, &c.

[5] *A System of Magic*, p. 125. In De Foe's *Political History of the Devil*, p. 225, occurs *apoplectic*, for 'apoplectic attack'. Compare *hectic*.

[6] In these cases,—to which is added *juvenile*, for 'child',—we are told, "the thing is deprived of its substantive name, and designated by an unessential, accidental quality". If it be unessential and accidental to a *philosopher* and to a *child* to be *philosophic* and *juvenile*, respectively, what is essential to them?

[7] One of the objections urged against *editorial*, for 'leader' or 'leading article', is "its conversion of an adjective, not signifying a quality, as *good* or *ill*, into a noun". It would be curious to have a classification of adjectives by Mr. White.

Despite the impressment which *ill* here suffers, the word is not, to Mr. White, a proper adjective. A few pages forward, I quote him to this effect.

Pastoral, whether meaning 'pastoral poem' or 'pastoral address', is just like *editorial*. The substantives *chemical, classic, contemporary, delf, domestic, epidemic, exotic, familiar, frolic, georgic, ideal, individual, lacteal, lyric, menial, mineral, narrative, official, particular, patent, recluse, rustic, vagrant, vernacular*, &c. &c., were, in like manner, born of ellipsis.

in vogue with our ancestors are now laid aside;[1] and we have, on the other hand, scores that were unknown to our ancestors. It is solely for usage, not for Mr. White, to stamp them as good, or as bad.

A castigation of the verb *donate* opens thus:

"I need hardly say that this word is utterly abominable,[2]—one that any lover of simple honest English cannot hear with patience and without offence. It has been formed, by some presuming and ignorant person, from *donation*, and is much such a word as *vocate* would be from *vocation*, *orate* from *oration*, or *gradate* from *gradation*."

Yet it is maintained that

"no man needs the authority of a dictionary (even such authority as dictionaries have), or of previous usage, for such a word as *juxtapose*. It is involved in *juxtaposition*, as much as *interpose* and *transpose* are in *interposition* and *transposition*."

One of the unavoidable inferences to which the reader is driven by these two extracts is, that Mr. White has an unreasonable distaste for one word, and an unreasonable disposition to patronize another. We gather, too, from these extracts, some fresh hints as to what he takes to be the pedigree of our words, no less theoretically than in fact. In the case of formal primitives and derivatives, we may speak of the latter as "involved" in the former; but it is unphilosophical and, often, practically absurd to speak of the former as "involved" in the latter. *Juxtapose*, Mr. White teaches, is "involved" in *juxtaposition;* and he thinks he settles the point by an appeal to analogy. By this sort of reasoning, *cond* and *trad* are "involved" in *condition* and *tradition*, because we have *addition* and *add*.[3]

---

[1] Many of these were almost always used in the plural; as *additionals*, *conjecturals*, *considerables*, *dissolutes*, *equivocals*, *ignorants*, *illiterates*, *impossibles*, *memorables*, *miserables*, *observables*, *probables*, *remarkables*, *sensibles*, *speculatives*. Like these are our *incurables*, &c.

[2] Violent language of this stamp repels rather than converts. Mr. De Quincey writes, in a like strain: "*Actual*, in the sense of 'present', is one of the most frequent, but also of the most disgusting, Gallicisms." *Logic of Political Economy*, p. 122, foot-note. I am not going to advocate for this sense of *actual;* but it is worth noting that it occurs in the pages of Junius, Gibbon, Burke, Lord Broughton, and Dr. Arnold.

[3] It is long since our language passed out of the stage during which words like *add* were introduced into it. From *condere* and *tradere* we should now form, if we required them, *condit* and *tradit*. Compare our late *edit*. From the artificial *juxtaponere* we should regularly get *juxtaposit*, a word used by

And why, pray, on Mr. White's principles, is not the "utterly abominable" *donate* "involved" in *donation*? To him, *donate* should be a word of unexceptionable genealogy. The hypothetical "*gradate* from *gradation*" he places on a par with "*orate* from *oration*". Philology of this description it is difficult to discuss seriously. As none but the veriest tyro has to be apprised, *gradate* is directly in breach of analogy, whereas *orate* strictly conforms to analogy. Southey has used this verb in the *Quarterly Review*;[1] and we may be sure that he did not go, for it, to *oration*, but to the supine of *orare*; as Shelley, for his verb *festinate*,[2] went to the supine of *festinare*. Mr. White, however, inculcates,[3] that, in order to form a verb, "going to the Greek root of a Greek word from which an English

---

Derham. *Juxtapose*—the French have *juxtaposer*—is Gallic; and modern verbs on the model to which it conforms are exceptional. I have often heard the word in conversation, and seen it in print.

Those who venture to reason about the generation of words should look well to their general principles.

"If every word", says William Taylor, of Norwich, "that can be found in print is, therefore, sterling English, our language is at the mercy, not only of every bungler in composition, but of every compositor's bungling. Shakespeare may circulate false coin, and often does; and good money may have escaped the record of any authority. Let us rather ask, concerning a word, whether it has legitimate parentage, relations, descendants. If so, it is English, though it may never have found a printer for midwife." *Monthly Magazine*, Vol. 11 (1801), p. 290.

Taylor, in thus enunciating his test of what is English, confounds, in the same category, the actual and the potential. A century since, *deodorize* and *photograph*, now English in esse, were English only in posse. But let us apply Taylor's test. *Rumpere* has relations in abundance, fully recognized, as *abrupt*, *interruption*, *corruptness*; and, for descendants, it counts *rupture* and *rout*. Yet, in spite of relations, descendants, and legitimate parentage, the theoretic *rupt*, for 'break', is not English. As little, too, are *curr*, *pell*, *turb*, and their unnaturalized brethren innumerable. In deciding whether a word is analogically fitted to be English, we may dispense with asking whether it has ever had existence; but the question whether it is English, good or bad, cannot be entertained abstractedly from its present currency. Neither, in passing, does the nummulary metaphor of Taylor go quite on all fours. What he calls "good money" may be wrought into such; but, until so wrought, it is nothing but honest bullion.

"These are ani-mad-versions indeed, when a writer's words are madly *verted*, inverted, perverted against his true intent, and their grammaticall sense." Fuller, *The Appeal*, &c., Part 3, p. 21.

Agreeably to Taylor's dictum, by reason of *vertere*, *convert*, *advertence*, *vertical*, &c., *vert* is an English verb, not simply potentially, but actually.

[1] Vol. 37 (1828), p. 574. In leaders in the *Times* newspaper I have repeatedly seen *perorate*. Mr. De Quincey—*Works*, Vol. 6, p. 329,—has *spectate*: and who can believe that he went anywhere but to *spectare* for it?

[2] *Shelley Memorials*, p. 35.

[3] P. 208.

noun had already been formed" is an "illogical process". What is true of going to Greek roots must be true of going to Latin roots; and *affiliate* and *locate*, which have become English within the last hundred years, are, therefore, words of very dubious respectability. For, if not due to an "illogical process", they must be due to the "presuming and ignorant" who took them from *affiliation* and *location*. Parallel to *orate*, *festinate*, *affiliate*, and *locate* is *donate*, regularly educible from the supine of *donare*. And how does Mr. White know that "it has been formed, by some presuming and ignorant person, from *donation*"?[1] Has he discovered its inventor, and been told by him how it was generated? Nor is *donate* mere surplusage. Far from it, if used discriminatively, it would be a genuine accession to our language. As we *contribute* contributions, *subscribe* subscriptions, and *give* ordinary gifts, why should not we *donate* money, clothes, &c., on the occasions when we make what are specifically known as 'donations'? And very like *donate* is *eventuate*. *Event* has no true synonym; *eventuate* expresses an idea not otherwise expressible by a single word; and, as per-

---

[1] As an etymologist, Mr. White is always Mr. White. Criticizing Pollok's *unrepentable*, he objects, as fatal to it, that "there is no verb *unrepent*". Nor is there a verb *unaccount;* and, therefore, he is bound to contend, *unaccountable* is false English.

Again, to get a word meaning "make enthusiastic", Mr. White tells us: "From the Greek adjective *enthous*, an English verb, *enthuse*, might be properly formed". How he works out this conclusion is shrewdly left to conjecture. He says, indeed, in his Preface: "The few suggestions which I have made in etymology I put forth with no affectation of timidity, but with little concern as to their fate"; and the assurance and indifference thus professed are just such as, in default of sound scholarship, might be expected.

Seeing how Mr. White holds words to be deduced, one is not surprised to find him going astray, when he leaves the beaten track of phraseology. Thus, he writes, at p. 244: "Something of the same sort is done by the jocular *feminization* of the word Hebrew, and the calling a woman of that race a Shebrew." *Feminization* is all right, as connected with *femina;* and so would *marization* be, as connected with *mas;* but, as a word, though it may be *feminine*, cannot be a *female*, the proper term, here, is *femininization*,—like *naturalization*, not *naturization*.

Embryotic, also,—a word used by Sterne, I find,—Mr. White takes under his patronage, at p. 82. Our simplest adjective of ἔμβρυον would have been *embryous*, from ἔμβρυος, like *amphibious* from ἀμφίβιος: and add Milton's *atheous*, with *acephalous*, *analogous*, *anomalous*, *monotonous*, *synonymous*, *tyrannous*, &c. &c. But the modern Latinists, in adopting the form *embryo*, and declining it like *sermo* and *pulmo*, prepared the way for the adjective *embryonic;* and we shall do well, if, with Coleridge and others, we are satisfied with it.

tains to its form, it sorts with *accentuate* and *graduate. Eventuate* justified, *eventuation* is justified inclusively.

Regarding *execute*, we read:

> "A vicious use of this word has prevailed so long, become so common, that, although it produces sheer nonsense, there is little hope of its reformation, except in case of that rare occurrence in the history of language, a vigorous and persistent effort, on the part of the best speakers and writers and professional teachers, toward the accomplishment of a special purpose. The perversion referred to is the use of *executed* to mean 'hanged', 'beheaded', 'put to death'."

And the final decision, after much inanity which it is needless to repeat, is, that of this use "there is no justification; its only palliation being that afforded by custom and bad example."

Like the French *exécuter*, our *execute*, 'accomplish', 'make an end of', has passed to signify, when applied to a criminal, 'put an end to judicially'. Universal consent has so willed it; and it would be a mere waste of ink and paper to do more than remark the egregious inapplicability of the term "sheer nonsense" to that which has ten thousand parallels in language, which the most careful writers authorize, and which nobody can possibly misunderstand.[1] Who finds any fault with *forgive*, or with *pardon*, applied to 'an offence'?

> "*Fellowship*, used as a verb (for example, 'An attempt to *disfellowship* an evil, but to *fellowship* the evil-doer'), is an abomination which has been hitherto regarded as of American origin. . . . . To this use of *fellowship* it would be a perfect parallel to say that, 'Fifteen years ago, the monarchs of Europe would not *kingship* with Louis Napoleon'. . . . Words ending in *ship* express a condition or state; and *fellowship* means the condition or state of those who are *fellows*, or who *fellow* with each other."

In all languages, abstract words largely come to be concretes, aggregative or particular. Familiar instances are seen in *Christendom* and *laity*. *Rascality* once meant 'rascals'; *nobility* has, for one of its meanings, 'collective nobles'; similar are *knighthood*, *magistracy*, and *peerage;*

---

[1] *Executioner*, which we use in only one sense, would pass clean out of our language, under Mr. White's purification of it.

talent and *genius* may signify 'men of talent' and 'men of genius'; &c. &c. *Notability*, for 'notable person', is as old as Chaucer; and we all speak of *celebrities, mediocrities,* and *notorieties*. Add our *affinities, antiquities, charities, facilities,* &c., almost without end. *Fellowship* once had the sense of 'society', 'kindred host', as is proved by the *Te Deum;* [1] and, when it had acquired this signification, it was just as eligible a candidate for metamorphosis into a verb, as *band, club, crowd, herd,* or *throng*. *Kingship* was never in like manner qualified. *Worship*, the verb from the substantive, affords a strict parallel to the verb *fellowship*, which, however odious from association of ideas, is entirely a legitimate development; and *disworship*, an old mongrel verb from *worship*, gives security for *disfellowship*.[2]

Under the heading of *gratuitous*, it is written:

"An affected use of this word has, of late, become too common. It is used in the various senses 'unfounded', 'unwarranted', 'unreasonable', 'untrue', no one of which can be given to it with propriety. It is not thus used either by the cultivated, or by those who speak plain English in a plain way, they know not why or how, and who are content to call a spade a spade. *Gratuitous* means 'without payment'; as, for instance, 'Professor A. delivered a *gratuitous* lecture'. . . . . True, dictionaries are found in which *gratuitous* is defined as meaning 'asserted without proof or reason'. But, in a moment's reflection, any intelligent person will see that *gratuitous* cannot mean 'asserted', in any manner. Dictionaries have come to be, in too many cases, the pernicious record of unreasonable, unwarranted, and fleeting usage."

Even in Cicero, *gratuitus* signifies 'voluntary', 'spontaneous', 'free'; [3] nothing is more natural than the de-

---

[1] "The goodly *fellowship* of the prophets praise thee". In Mr. Palmer's *Origines Liturgicæ* (ed. 1845), Vol. 1, p. 258, the original runs: "Te prophetarum laudabilis *numerus*." "Laudat" is suspended, and is to be resumed from the versicle next succeeding.

For *fellowship*, in the sense of 'company', also see Pecock's *Repressor*, pp. 376, 377; and Capgrave's *Chronicle*, pp. 159, 217, 225, 226, 239, 246, 289.

[2] Compare, as a mongrel, *dishearten*. Our older literature swarms with words like *disbrother, discloud, disman, disstream*.

[3] This sense *gratuitous*, also, has had.

"Petrarch was a delicate man, and, with an elegant judgment, *gratuitously* confined love within the limits of honour, wit within the bounds of discretion, eloquence within the terms of civility", &c. Gabriell Harvey, *Pierce's Supererogation*, p. 61.

generation of freedom into lawless licence; and we thus see how a word that began with meaning 'without reward' came to mean 'unauthorized', &c.[1] And what reader of our literature is ignorant of the use of *gratis* for 'groundlessly', &c.?[2] As for language used by "the cultivated", and quite free from the blemish of being "affected", it appears that Mr. White stands unique in knowing where to look for it. Let it lurk where it may, the latest use of *gratuitous* and its adverb, execrable as he deems it, is good enough for Bishop Warburton,[3] John-

"All our powers and faculties, all the properties and perfections of our nature, were *gratuitously* given us by the good-will of our Maker, without our own asking or knowing." Dr. Richard Bentley, *Works* (ed. Rev. Alexander Dyce), Vol. 3, p. 264.

"How much he [Pope] was pleased with his *gratuitous* defender [Warburton], the following letter evidently shows." Johnson, *Life of Pope.*

"His Grace, like an able orator, as he is, begins with giving me a great deal of praise for talents which I do not possess. He does this, to intitle himself, on the credit of this *gratuitous* kindness", &c. Burke, *Letter to William Elliot, Esq.*

[1] So it meant, with us, more or less frequently, even before Queen Anne's time. See Dr. Johnson's *Dictionary.*

The signification in question has long been borne by the French *gratuit.* I here quote from Richelet (ed. 1732): "*Gratuit* signifie, en termes de Philosophie, qui n'a aucun fondement. C'est une suposition *gratuite.*" Again: "*Gratuitement* signifie . . sans fondement. Vous avancez cela *gratuitement.*" See M. Littré, for pertinent extracts from Buffon, Montesquieu, Voltaire, and d'Alembert.

In Italian, *grato* "talvolta vale senza occasione, senza motivo". Cardinali.

[2] "Rather should their forwardness to judge thus uncharitably of us make us to walk the more warily and wisely, not to give them cause . . . . that, if yet they will needs speak evil of us, as of evil doers, they may do it *gratis*, and to their own shame, and not ours." Bishop Sanderson, *Works,* Vol. 2, p. 64. The passage is from a sermon preached in 1636.

"That I allow not Euclid this axiom *gratis*, ... you know to be untrue." Hobbes, *Works*, Vol. 7, p. 228. Also see pp. 257, 263.

"For, first, he . . . . believes *gratis*, without any ground of his supposal." Glanvill, *Scire Tuum Nihil Est* (ed. 1665), p. 38. Also see Glanvill's *Essays*, &c., II., p. 39; V., p. 24; VI., p. 2.

"But, with regard to the increase, the matter is very different. It is all his own; the public is loaded (for anything we can see to the contrary) entirely *gratis.*" Burke, *Observations on a late 'State of the Nation'.*

"Lord Shelburne had told me *gratis* (for nothing led to it), that the people . . . . were never in the wrong", &c. *Idem, Correspondence,* Vol. 2, p. 111.

Since the middle ages, *gratis dictum* has been a common expression; and "vous dites cela *gratis*" has long been good French.

"But was not this *gratis dictum* of Abraham?" Fuller, *Mixt Contemplations in Better Times*, XLII.

"It is *gratis dictum*." Abp. Manning, *The Unity of the Church*, p. 145. Also see Mason, in *The School for Satire*, p. 41.

[3] "Had the sabbatarian interpretation of this sanctification of the seventh

son,[1] Burke,[2] Paley,[3] Porson,[4] Godwin,[5] Hazlitt,[6] Charles Lamb,[7] Southey,[8] Dr. Arnold,[9] Sydney Smith,[10] Lord Macaulay,[11] Mr. De Quincey,[12] and Dr. Newman.[13]

"*Grow* is even more perverted than *get* is, in vulgar use, although the misapplications of it are not so numerous. It is

---

day been the true, it must have followed it must have been observed, by the people of God, from the creation to the giving of the Law. And so, indeed, the sabbatarians say it was; but they say it *gratuitously*, and, what is worse, falsely." *A Selection from Unpublished Papers*, &c. (1841), pp. 274, 275.

1 "The story of reducing his exuberance . . . . seems to have been *gratuitously* transferred to Milton." *Life of Milton*.

2 "But, as these occasions may never arrive, the mind receives a *gratuitous* taint", &c. *Reflections on the Revolution in France.*

3 Their sportive motions, their wanton mazes, their *gratuitous* activity, their continual change of place", &c. *Natural Theology*, Ch. 26.

4 In short, Vigilius's claims to either of these publications are only supported by some weak and *gratuitous* conjectures of Chifflet." *Letters to Mr. Archdeacon Travis*, p. 339.

5 "A *gratuitous* assumption." *The Enquirer* (1797), p. 13.

6 *Lectures on the English Comic Writers*, pp. 52, 83, 372: *Table-talk*, Vol. 1, p. 226; Vol. 2, pp. 349, 372.

7 *Letters*, &c., Vol. 2, p. 136.

8 "Therapeutics were in a miserable state as long as practitioners proceeded upon the *gratuitous* theory of elementary complections." *Colloquies*, Vol. 1, p. 254. Also see *Omniana*, Vol. 2, p. 329; *Life of Wesley*, Vol. 2, p. 198; and *Cowper's Works*, Vol. 2, pp. 114, 288.

9 *Life and Correspondence* (ed. 1846), pp. 300, 546, 551: *Miscellaneous Works*, p. 477.

10 "The imprisonment of a poor man, because he cannot find bail, is not a *gratuitous* vexation, but a necessary severity." *Works* (one-vol. ed., London, 1850), p. 55.

11 "Supposing quite *gratuitously*". First article on Sadler: *Edinburgh Review*, Vol. 51 (1830), p. 313.

12 "The story was a pure, *gratuitous* invention of his own". *Works*, Vol. 12, p. 45.

13 "But it is needless to dwell on the improbability of an hypothesis which has been shown to be altogether *gratuitous*". *Essay on the Miracles*, &c., p. 169.

"This *gratuitous* insinuation": "his *gratuitous* accusation". *Apologia pro Vita Sua*, Appendix, pp. 9, 66. Qualifying "hypothesis", "assumption", "gloss". *Essays Critical and Historical*, Vol. 1, pp. 32, 63, 206; *Discussions and Arguments on Various Subjects*, pp. 169, 370, 381, 382, 384.

I may as well add, here, a passage from Bentley, in which *gratuitously* is used precisely as Cicero uses *gratuito*, namely, in the sense of 'for no particular reason'. "But there is a learned Greek professor . . . . who, after he has asserted the credit of Euripides's Letters, *gratuitously* undertakes to apologize for these, too, about this matter of the dialect." *Works*, Vol. 1, p. 159.

The great Grecian's puny antagonist, the Hon. Charles Boyle, adverting to the word italicized, "can make no other sense of it" than "without having anything for his pains", and subjoins: "This looks as if the Dr. thought learned men were to set a price upon their civilities, and never part with a favour till they had their fee." Bentley, with just scorn, speaks of this as "a sorry, but yet a very spiteful, quibble, . . . which is a privileged slander, and cannot, with good manners, be answered in the manner it deserves."

used in the sense of 'become'. Such phrases are constantly heard as 'the smooth sea *grew* rough', 'the clear sky *grew* black', 'the coat had *grown* soiled', and even 'the moon *grows* smaller after the full', or 'the chances are *growing* smaller day by day'. Now, *grow* means 'increase', 'the enlargement of a present quality or condition', not 'a change, in character, of that quality or condition'. A rough sea may *grow* rougher, a dark sky *grow* black; but a smooth sea *becomes* rough, a clear sky *becomes* black, a coat *becomes* soiled, and the moon, or anything else that lessens, does not *grow*, but *becomes*, smaller."

Immediately after the passage just quoted, Mr. White speaks of the objection to *help*, in the sense of 'avoid', as "a good example of a prim, precise treatment of language, that would deprive it of all strength and flexibility. There is no better English than 'I can't help it', which is a compact and homely way of saying 'the matter is beyond my aid'." On precisely the same footing with this use of *help* stands *grow*, to import 'become'; only Mr. White has taken a fancy to the one, and has taken an aversion to the other. The latter, as being an object of his dislike, belongs, of course, to "vulgar use". If it ought to be discarded, we should likewise discard '*go* mad', '*run* wild', '*fall* sick', '*get* well',[1] '*wax* angry', &c. &c. Among the writers at whom Mr. White unconsciously knits his austere brows, and whom he consigns to the rank of vulgarians, are Dr. Johnson and Lord Macaulay. For the first writes "*grew* acquainted", "*grew* less pleased", and "*grow* rich";[2] and the latter, "*grow* smaller" and "must be *growing* a fine girl".[3]

It is singular how even men of generally good judgment sometimes allow their fancy to get the upper hand.

---

[1] Mr. White probably rejects this idiom, since he debars "*getting* crazy". Yet Dr. Johnson, in his *Life of Dorset*, writes "*got* drunk".

[2] *Idler*, Nos. 64, 69. Elsewhere, Johnson has "*grow* fewer", "*grew* able", "*grow* less", "*grown* desirous", "*grows* little". *Works* (Murphy's ed., 1816), Vol. 2, pp. 33, 231, 304; Vol. 11, p. 123; Vol. 12, p. 260.

[3] *Speeches*, &c., p. 55: *History*, Chapter 20. In his *Essay on Ranke's History of the Popes*, Lord Macaulay writes: "The zeal of the Catholics *waxed* cool".

Steele has "to *grow* less". *Guardian*, No. 76.

Bishop Lowth has "*grown* poor". *Life of William of Wykeham*, p. 300.

Gray has "we *grew* the best acquaintance," and "*grow* less". *Works*, Vol. 2, p. 174; Vol. 4, p. 172.

Bentham, equally with Mr. White, has his favourite horrors. Listen to him:[1]

"*Besides*, and *again*, and *this too*, and *moreover*,—it is by words of this sort that the symptom of weakness, here called fumbling, is betrayed."

Herein the philosopher forgets, for once, to be philosophic. Inasmuch as, when under the temptation to use the expressions which he enumerates, he felt himself to be fumbling, it was right and becoming that he avoided them; to fumble being, to his mind, vicious. At the same time, it was somewhat despotic in him to demand that his own consciousness in the matter ought to be the consciousness of everybody else. Again, or besides, or moreover,—and yet I am not aware that I fumble,—how constantly, on the showing of the great jurisprudent, we who have written English have, all of us, been fumbling, for several centuries. Though, in tacit profession, launching a shaft at loose morality, Bentham really aims, in his denunciation, at an established usage which nothing but blind prejudice would ever think of excepting against.

To say 'a man is *ill*', or to speak of the proverbial '*ill* wind' or '*ill* weeds', of 'a house of *ill* fame', or of '*ill* health', '*ill* luck', '*ill* will', is, to Mr. White's thinking, not to be endured. "For the use of *ill*, an adverb, as an adjective,[2]—thus, 'an *ill* man',—there is no defence and no excuse, except the contamination of bad example." In our day, the expression instanced is not used in any sense; but yet, just as much as there, *ill*, before whatever substantive, is an adjective. That this word, a contraction of *evil*, was originally an adverb is a fiction for the nonce; and, even if it had been at first an adverb, has not usage converted the adverb *forward* into an adjective, and even into a verb? Moreover, if *ill* be not a proper adjective, *illness*[3] can hardly be a proper substantive. The "bad

[1] *Works* (ed. Sir John Bowring), Vol. 8, p. 308.

[2] At p. 74, note[7], we have seen that Mr. White adduces *ill*, with *good*, as a normal adjective.

The adverb *illy*—occasionally used in America, and of which Mr. Wright, in his *Dictionary of Obsolete and Provincial English*, gives an instance under the date of 1604,—and the old *smally*, could never become popular. It takes too long to pronounce them.

[3] Mr. Ruskin, in *Unto This Last*, p. 126, proposes *illth*, as antithetical to

example" which we are told of has been working its "contamination" ever since the thirteenth century, and, probably, longer. Better than in the extract just quoted, Mr. White has nowhere displayed, in a short compass, the extravagance of his whimsicality, his recklessness of facts, and his exorbitant intolerance.

Not unlike Mr. White's position regarding *ill* is that of Cobbett regarding *than whom:*

"'Cromwell, *than whom* no man was better skilled in artifice'. A hundred such phrases might be collected from Hume, Blackstone, and even from Doctors Blair and Johnson. Yet they are bad grammar. In all such cases, *who* should be made use of; for it is nominative, and not objective." [1]

There is nothing, in this decision, of Cobbett's usual independence of his brother-grammarians of English. Ordinarily, his attitude towards them is that of scornful dissent; and any careful student of their vagaries can have little confidence in a race who, to judge from the outcome of their labours, seem, in most cases, to have qualified themselves for their duties by merely learning a little Latin, and purging themselves of common sense. Or was it that the attractions of general dissidence here prevailed, with Cobbett, over the attractions of special dissidence? Did he here side with the grammarians, because they furnished him with a weapon against universal custom? Be this as it may, the grammarians posit the absence of regimen as one of the differential features of a conjunction; herein Cobbett concurs with them; and, therefore, we should write: "Cromwell, *than who* no man was better skilled in artifice". That any one but Cobbett would abide this, as English, is highly improbable; and how the expression, a quite classical one, which he discards can be justified grammatically, except by calling its *than* a preposition, others may resolve at their leisure and pleasure.[2] Cobbett, and so Mr. White,

---

wealth; and, in *Fors Clavigera*, Letter 7, p. 13, he opposes *common-illth* to *common-wealth*.

Lithgow uses *well* for 'welfare'. "The soyle of Hungary aboundeth infinitly in all things the earth can produce for the *well* of man". *The Totall Discourse*, &c., p. 414.

[1] *A Grammar of the English Language*, § 200. That which Cobbett gives as a reason must, in order to become such, be construed sylleptically.

[2] According to the analogy of the Latin, we ought to say 'He is older than

treats English much in the manner of a tailor who, instead of making new coats after the measure of his customers, should pare down his customers to fit coats ready-made.

"Many women, and even some men, who should know better, are in the habit of speaking of their *jewelry*, when they mean their *jewels*. The word thus used is of very low caste. . . . . As applied to trinkets and precious stones, the word means, at best, 'jewels in general', not any particular jewels. It is of very late introduction, in any sense; not being in Shakespeare, or the Bible, or Milton, or in Johnson's Dictionary. . . . But, properly, 'jewels' are no more *jewelry* than 'shrubs' are *shrubbery*, 'slaves' *slavery*, or 'beggars' *beggary*. *Jewelry* is, properly, the name of the place in which jewels are kept; as *slavery* is the name of the condition in which slaves are kept; as *beggary* is that of the condition in which beggars are; and as *shrubbery* is that of grounds filled with shrubs. These words belong to a numerous class ending in *ry*, which express place, or condition, which is moral place."

A larger variety of superficial philology than is here exhibited could not easily be condensed within the space which it occupies. Our termination *-ery*, often euphonically shortened to *-ry*,[1] came to us, directly, from the French *-erie*, which frequently denotes a collection. *Artillery*, *cavalry*, *chicanery*, *chivalry*, *frippery*, *infantry*, *musketry*, *napery*, for instance, we took, essentially made to our hands, from the French; and we have coined *ancestry*, *blazonry*, *enginery*, *imagery*,[2] *knicknackery*, *pageantry*, *poultry*, *scenery*, *soldiery*, *tenantry*, *tracery*, *yeomanry*, &c. &c., ourselves.[3] In all languages, abstracts are readily trans-

---

me'. But we should have to make our language over, from the beginning, if we would have it quadrate with other languages. 'That man is *he*' accords with the Latin, and yet not with the French, &c. 'That man is *him*', it is contended by many, is preferable. One or other of the forms will eventually be ousted, but by usage, and by usage alone.

[1] To other classes of words belong *baptistery*, *directory*, *legendary*, *presbytery*, *psaltery*, *statuary*, *treasury*, &c. &c. *Fairy* was, originally, a collective.

[2] *Ymagoure*, our earliest form of *imagery*, meaning 'images', occurs in *Kyng Alysaunder*, which was written in the thirteenth century. See Weber's *Metrical Romances*, Vol. 1, p. 313. Pecock, in his *Repressor*, pp. 139 and 144, has *ymagerie* and *ymagirie*.

[3] Shakespeare has *villagery*, for 'collection of villages'; Richard Brathwait, *infantry*, for 'infants'. Milton uses *Irishry*; and so does Lord Macaulay, with *Englishry* and *helotry* (helots). Horace Walpole has *giantry* and *riotry* (rioters); Charles Lamb, *citizenry*, *girlery*, *pantaloonery*; Southey, *cattery*, *rascalry*, *trinketry*; Coleridge, *branchery*; William Taylor, *angelry*, *valetry*,

formed into concretes; and, hence, such words as *draperie*, *épicerie*, and *mercerie*, at first, 'cloth-trade', &c., from *drapier*, *épicier*, and *mercier*, came to mean the articles in which these traffickers deal. Setting out with the secondary sense of words like those enumerated, in their English forms *drapery*, *spicery*, and *mercery*, we have come by our *braziery*,[1] *cutlery*, *haberdashery*, *hosiery*, *millinery*, *peddlery*, *perfumery*, *saddlery*, *upholstery*,[2] &c. &c.; and the analogy followed, in framing them, is so well established, that we do not hesitate to increase their number, as we have occasion. Accordingly, whether taken as an English formative, or as a naturalized exotic, our *jewellery*[3] is religiously analogical. When, therefore, a lady speaks of her *jewellery*, her language is every particle as proper as is that of a landlord in speaking of his *tenantry*[4]; and this

---

vassalry; Mr. Ruskin, *legendry* and *serpentry*; the Rev. Charles Kingsley, *studentry*; and I have seen *felonry*, for 'felons', in the *Saturday Review*. *Waggonry* is used contemptuously, by Milton, for *waggon*; and many an old writer has *harlotry* for *harlot*.

Such is our propensity to give words in *-ry* an aggregative sense, that, in domesticating *ménagerie*, we have changed its only present French sense, 'place where strange animals are collected', and apply it to the animals themselves.

[1] "For example, ... navigation, from Zebulun; *brazery*, or smith-works, from Tubal Cain; musick, from Jubal". Brathwait, *The English Gentleman*, &c., p. 72.

[2] *Vide supra*, p. 30, note [1].

[3] This, if we made the word ourselves, is, by analogy, a better form than *jewelry*; for, as we have seen, things that may be objects of trade are denoted collectively by adding *-y*—a euphonic shortening of *-ry*,—to the appellative of their appropriate tradesman.

Early in the last century, *joüalerie* (now *joaillerie*) was defined "marchandise de joüalier". M. Littré has: "Des articles de *joaillerie*".

[4] "*Jewelry*", with "*confectionary*, *pastry*, and *crockery*", Mr. White calls "words which have been perverted by careless speakers". These,—a sort of reservation being made in favour of the last,—and also *pottery*, he indirectly advises to be turned out of the language. For the retention of "*jewelry*," *pastry*, and *pottery*, nothing can be pleaded, he says, "except conformity to a bad custom which perverts meaning, cramps language, and violates analogy".

Mr. White writes *confectionary*,—a spelling which should have led him to look elsewhere than to *confectioner*, for its origin. And so write most English dictionaries, though English usage now knows no spelling but *confectionery*. *Confectionary*, from the Low Latin *confectionarius*, means, in Shakespeare and the Bible, *confectioner*; and Nash, Shakespeare's contemporary,—in his *Lenten Stuffe* (in the *Harleian Miscellany*, ed. Oldys and Park, Vol. 6, p. 158),—writes of "junquetries or *confectionaries*"; *confectionaries* here representing *confectionaria*. In Nash's *Christ's Tears*, &c., p. 140, written in 1594, we already find *confectioner*: Brathwait, in *A Boulster-lecture*, p. 160, has *confectioness*; and Henry Earl of Monmouth, the verb active *confec-*

use, "of very low caste" though Mr. White calls it,[1] has been accepted by Burke,[2] Landor,[3] Lord Macaulay,[4] Mr. De Quincey,[5] Mr. Ruskin,[6] and by our contemporaries universally.[7] In fact, nothing is wanting, Mr. White's simple 'placet' excepted, to raise it to the highest patrician rank.[8]

---

tionate. *Pensionary*, *primary*, and *proprietary* were succeeded by *pensioner*, *primer*, and *proprietor;* and *confectionary*, the personal substantive, was superseded by *confectioner*,—whence our *confectionery*. *Confectionary*, to us, is much as *stationary* would be, to designate the wares of a *stationer*. Contrariwise to *confectionary*, supplanted by *confectioner*, we first had *missioner*, and then, owing to the influence of the French *missionnaire*, *missionary*. *Missioner* is used even by Goldsmith and Horace Walpole; and Romanists still generally cling to the old word.

Crockery,—unless a collective of the old *crocke*, for *crock*,—is, probably, a like formation, and came from *crocker;* for the survival of the proper name so spelled almost proves that *crock* once had a personal derivative. *Pastry* and *pottery* were corrupted from the French; and the rule of our language, long ago established, in dealing with depravations of foreign words, is, to let them alone.

1 Addison writes, in the *Spectator*, No. 351: "I am apt to think that the changing of the Trojan fleet into water-nymphs, which is the most violent *machine* in the whole Æneid, and has given offence to several critics, may be accounted for the same way." When we talk of the *machinery* of a poem, do we mean anything but the plural of Addison's *machine ?*

2 As is noted by Mr. White, referring to Dr. Richardson's *Dictionary*.

3 *Last Fruit off an Old Tree*, pp. 4, 17, 346.

4 *Essays on the Comic Dramatists of the Restoration, on Warren Hastings, on Madame d'Arblay, and on Addison: History*, Chapter 10.

5 *Works*, Vol. 1, p. 86; Vol. 11, pp. 127, 136; Vol. 14, pp. 108, 162.

6 *The Seven Lamps of Architecture*, p. 32: *Lectures on Architecture and Painting*, p. 95.

7 In what follows, Mr. White, doubtless, conceives that he is making a point. "Think of Cornelia pointing to the Gracchi, and saying 'These are my *jewelry*'; or read thus a grand passage in the last of the Hebrew prophets: 'And they shall be mine, saith the Lord of hosts, in that day when I make up my *jewelry!*'" The effect is ludicrous, it must be granted. And so it is, if we read: 'I will make you *fishermen* of men'. Nevertheless, *fisherman* could, in most cases, be changed for *fisher*, only at the cost of affectation; and *jewellery*, in its place, which there is little difficulty in finding, is liable to no rational challenge.

8 So far was William Taylor from Mr. White's way of thinking, that he refused to use *rivalry* for *rivalship*, and contended, very erroneously, that it could properly signify 'rivals' only.

What Mr. White says of *beggary* and *slavery* is quite correct, as a statement of current usage; but what he says of *shrubbery* needs amendment. *Beggary* and *slavery* might, however, be decreed, by usage, with perfect regularity, to mean 'beggars' and 'slaves'.

I have by no means been contemplating all our categories of words in *-ery*, *-ry*, and *-y*. *Buttery* and many other similar words express 'place', certainly. But, among these, Mr. White mistakes in naming *grocery*, which, in the English of England, does not mean 'grocer's shop'.

Mr. White is not, however, invariably consistent in his somewhat overdone preference for the establishments of former times, or what he takes to be such. For example, his views of marrying are quite revolutionary. Some, he tells us, marry John Smith *to* Mary Jones; others denote the connexion by *with;* and others still, by *and.* "I have no hesitation in saying that all of these forms are incorrect. We know, indeed, what is meant by any one of them; but the same is true of hundreds and thousands of erroneous uses of language." It may be anticipated, that objection would be taken to the Scotch mode of marrying John Smith *upon* Mary Jones. What, then, is the correct thing? "The proper form of announcement is; Married, Mary Jones *to* John Smith." And the reason? "Properly speaking, a man is not married *to* a woman, or married *with* her; nor are a man and a woman married *with* each other. The woman is married *to* the man." "The etymology of the word agrees entirely with the conditions of the act which it expresses. To *marry* is to 'give', or to 'be given, to a husband', *mari.*"[1]

Hapless Mary Jones! John Smith, though by courtesy called her husband, is not, for all that, in any sense a *married* man. Neither, except so far as those who gave her away are concerned, is Mary Jones, according to Mr. White's definition of *marry,*[2] intelligibly a *married* woman. In *marrying* John, Mary is "given to a husband", to be sure; but, to justify the deluded victim in calling herself, save as aforesaid, *married,* we must ascertain for her a passive voice of *to be given,* itself passive. The '*married* state' must, further, be a 'state given in marriage'. There being, then, no married men, and, otherwise than

[1] The previous context is as follows: "'*Nubo: viro trador:* to be married to a man. For it is in the woman's part only'. *Lilly's Grammar.* In speaking of the ceremony, it is proper to say that he married her (*duxit in matrimonio*), and not that she married him, but that she was married to him." Here, as in many other places, Mr. White requires a commentator. To a plain understanding his reasoning is all at sixes and sevens. If "to *marry* is to 'give', or to 'be given to a husband'," how can a man marry a woman? Moreover, as he grounds his notion of the right use of *marry* on its etymology, his cheap Latin has about the same topical relevance that would belong to a receipt for making cream-cheese or a black-pudding.

[2] That definition, it will be observed, makes it as impossible for the parson as for John to *marry* Mary; for it is not his function to give the lady to a husband.

in a sort of Pickwickian sense, no married women either, free-lovers may, with good reason, look up.

Marry, in classical acceptation, has, with reference to the nuptial pair, all the extension of *wed;* and it is precisely as proper to speak of a man's *marrying* as to speak of his *marriage*. The word is, indeed, allied to the French *marier*, based on *mari*, 'husband'; but this fact is wholly inert as to determining our use of it. *Marier* denotes the act of giving away a bride, or that of performing the ceremony which gives her a husband; and *se marier* is said alike of the man and of the woman. Besides this, our *marry*, if it had come directly from *mari*, might, on the analogy of the verb *master*, have had the exclusive meaning 'become husband of'[1]; and *wive* might have meant 'become wife of'. But such considerations prove nothing. All the four senses which we give to *marry* are supported by the best writers; and the facts and figments brought forward by Mr. White are not of the slightest weight as against the decision of authoritative usage.[2]

"*Militate* is rarely misused, except that any use of it is misuse, and it belongs rather among words which are not words. . . . . What could be more absurd than the making of the Latin *milito* into an English word, to take the place of *oppose*, *contend*, *be at variance with*. . . . . The absurdity is the greater, because it is usually a supposition, or a theory, or something quite as incorporeal, that is *militated against*. The use of this word is, however, not a question of right or wrong, but one of taste. It belongs to a bad family, of which are *necessitate*, *ratiocinate*, *effectuate*, and *eventuate*, which, with their

---

1 As, likewise, we say that a man *husbands* property, or the like, in being a *husband*, 'economizer', of it; or that one man *rivals* another, in being his *rival*.

2 Just as this page is going to the press, I find the following in an English journal: "A new abomination has appeared in the United States vocabulary; *nuptiated*, for 'married'." Can this creation be in any way attributable to Mr. White's polemic against *marry?*

But *nuptiate*, except as being unneeded, is not quite an "abomination". *Exuviate*,—from *exuviæ*,—a word in good repute with naturalists, is just like it, as to genesis; and *exuviare* would not have shocked a Roman, as irregular. *Vide infra*, note [1] to p. 90..

If, when not content with *wed*, instead of going to the French for *marry*, we had gone to the Latin, we might have made, on the analogy of *divide*, *laud*, and *direct*, *nube*, *nub*, and *nupt*. As it is, we may congratulate ourselves on not *nupting* our daughters to suitors, and on our daughters' not *nubing* them.

substantives,—*necessitation*, *ratiocination*, *effectuation*, and *eventuation* (which must be received with their parent verbs),—should not be recognized as members of good English society."

At last, then, we are confronted with a

> Monstrum nulla virtute redemptum
> A vitiis.

Militate, moreover, "does not appear in Johnson's *Dictionary*". And what of that? Mr. White will hardly convert the world to his fashion of picking and choosing his words,

> "Like one well studied in a sad ostent
> To please his grandam."

Even if *militate*,[1] instead of dating from the seventeenth century,[2] were as modern as Mr. White supposes it to be, it would go very far towards being classicized by the sanction of Smollett,[3] Burke,[4] Jones of Nayland,[5]

---

[1] Sterne, in *Tristram Shandy*, Vol. 4, Ch. 22,—and Horace Walpole, likewise,—has *militiate*; and the Latins, instead of their *militare*, from *miles*, might have coined an original for it in *militiare*, from *militia*; as they made *furiare* and *luxuriare* from *furia* and *luxuria*.

[2] "I must now perform what I promis'd in the fourth place, namely, answer the arguments you apprehend to *militate* and fight against it." Burthogge, *Causa Dei* (1675), p. 151.

Mr. White thinks that *militate* "must have been creeping into newspaper-use in Johnson's day", and adds an instance from a journal "of more than ninety years ago". But what would it be against it, if it had first appeared in a newspaper? Words must be born into the world somewhere; and many a good one has, no doubt, originated from such a source. I have made but very slight quest for *militate* in writers more than a century old, as it seemed especially important to defend it, by appeals to usage, from the standing-point of taste. It is used by Sterne, in one of his letters, No. 17, written in 1761. The illustration adduced by Archdeacon Todd is from *The Confessional*, by Blackburne,—whose name Dr. Worcester corrupts into Blackstone,—published in 1767. The word occurs, too, in the preface to Robert Baker's *Remarks on the English Language*, ed. 1770. Smollett, who, also, uses *militate*, died in 1771.

[3] Dr. Webster is here my authority.

[4] "I shall not consider how forcibly this argument *militates* with their whole principle." *Speech on the Acts of Uniformity*, 1772.

"The tax . . . . *militates* with the assurance authentically conveyed to the colonies," &c. *Speech on American Taxation*, 1774.

"These are deep questions, where great names *militate* against each other." *Speech on Conciliation with America*, 1775.

These extracts all date "more than ninety years ago", and, however they may harmonize with the "newspaper-use" of that day, are from speeches delivered in Parliament. Seven other passages might be quoted, from Burke, where he uses *militate* followed by 'with'; and once he has "*militate* under", in his *Speech on the Nabob of Arcot's Debts*. For "*militate* against", see *The Epistolary Correspondence of Burke and Dr. Laurence*, pp. 103, 143.

It is pertinent to remark, that no one, until he has familiarized himself with the writings of Burke, should venture to discourse on modern English.

[5] "Sometimes they take a text independently, so as to make it *militate* against

Paley,[1] Southey,[2] Coleridge,[3] Mr. De Quincey,[4] Landor,[5] and Dr. Newman.[6] Its original, *militare*, signifies 'serve as a soldier', 'strive', from which its own acceptation does not vary much.[7] To give it, with respect to its etymology, the meaning it now bears is "absurd",[8] just as much as our modern *consul, gazette, journal, outlandish, preposterous,*

---

the tenour of the divine law." *Theological and Miscellaneous Works*, Vol. 2, p. 243. This was written between 1771 and 1773. Two similar instances are seen in Vol. 6, p. 126.

1 In six instances, at least, Paley uses *militate* followed by 'with'; once, followed by 'against', viz., in his Moral *Philosophy*, Book 4, Chapter 3.

2 *Letters*, &c. (1797), p. 273.

3 *Essays on His Own Times*, pp. 344, 472, 833.

4 *Works*, Vol. 9, p. 216. "*Militated* for", there used of the Roman Republic, signifies 'fought for'. As I learn from M. Littré, *militer*, in the fifteenth century, signified 'to be a soldier'.

Hobbes uses *fight* figuratively. "These propositions *fight* not only against the King of England, but against all the kings of the world." *Works*, Vol. 6, p. 353. Compare the extract in note [2], p. 90.

5 *Last Fruit off an Old Tree*, p. 163.

6 *Apologia pro Vita Sua*, p. 332.

7 The French formerly employed *militer* with both *contre* and *pour* or *en faveur de*; at present, it appears, it is constructed with the latter only. *Militare*, in Italian, now generally follows the surviving French use. And this use has been imitated in English. Bishop Horne writes: "His example *militates* powerfully *in favour of* the plan." *Olla Podrida*, No. 12. Mr. Kett, in No. 39 of the same periodical, also employs *militate*.

8 The Romans used *impugnare* and *repugnare*, except that the first is always active, precisely as we use *militate*.

More than once it happened to me, when living in India, to fall in with an enthusiast who, by dint of daily perusing his omphalic node for six or eight hours on end, constantly repeating the words 'Râm, Râm', the while, had ended with hearing the music of the spheres, scenting the lotoses of the celestial Ganges, and enjoying the beatific vision of Krishna and his multitudinous paramours. In like manner, any person of ill-conditioned mind may, no doubt, by persevering contemplation of almost anything, bring himself to believe it quite the reverse of what it seems to that healthful and unclouded reason which allows to dry and sober facts the consideration they deserve.

A good sample of Mr. White's inexactness is seen in his defining the neuter *militate* by "be at variance with", a phrase essentially tantamount to a verb active. This by the way. As to its being "absurd" to make *militare* into *militate*, why it is not equally so to transfigure any other Latin verb into an English verb is a matter which Mr. White reserves, seemingly, as part of his esoteric discipline. And in what does a Latin participle differ, as a subject for importation into our language, from a Latin verb, in case he allows the expression 'church *militant*'? Again, because, among the Romans, only men *militated*, suppositions and theories, it appears, are not to take, with us, a liberty unknown two thousand years ago in Italy. By this rule, a fashion may not *dominate* or *predominate*, be *dominant* or *predominant*; and it is not at all clear how *Words and Their Uses*, since the book has not material legs to propel it, can be a '*leading* authority', with certain sons and daughters of the thoughtless.

puny, uncouth, and *viands* are "absurd"; and, in our making its object "a supposition, or a theory, or something quite as incorporeal", "the absurdity is the greater", pretty much as it is when we talk of '*corroborating* a statement', or of 'the *boundary-line* between wisdom and folly', the overstepping of which we have not to go far to see exemplified. And what objection, free from fatuity, or prompted by anything but intellectual emasculation, can be brought against *necessitate, ratiocinate, effectuate,*[1] and their conjugates?[2] Most of them the best of our writers have employed for two hundred years and more; and, short of tedious periphrases, we have nothing to take their places. *Eventuate* and *eventuation* I have already remarked on.[3]

Obnoxious, as in "to change *obnoxious*", and the like, Mr. White would be glad to see revived; this use of it being fast on the wane.[4] Its suggestion of *noxious*[5] told against it; and, for an analogous reason, the older sense of *impertinent* is rapidly falling into disuse. No sense of *obnoxious* but that of "liable or exposed to harm" was known, says Mr. White, "until the close of the last century; as may be seen by reference to Richardson's *Dictionary*": and, in so saying, he makes two gross mistakes. Long before the year 1800, *obnoxious* had the sense which it now most generally has, and also senses of which Mr. White knows nothing.[6] Even from Dr. Johnson we learn that it was used,

---

[1] The Italian has *necessitare, raziocinare,* and *effettuare;* the French, *nécessiter, ratiociner,* and *effectuer.*

[2] It is rarely any but bad models that Mr. White can be compared to. Extremely like his perturbation at polysyllables is the feeling evinced, in the following passage, by a gentleman whom it is not much of a venture to term the "inspired idiot" of the nineteenth century. "And, at this day, though I have kind invitations enough to visit America, I could not, even for a couple of months, live in a country so miserable as to possess no castles." Mr. John Ruskin, *Fors Clavigera,* Letter 10, p. 9.

[3] *Vide supra,* pp. 77, 78.

[4] Here, as with reference to *controvertist,* Mr. White figures in the unfavourable character of a conservatist just for the sake of conservatism. The annexed observation of Bishop Sprat may pertinently be recommended to his consideration. "There is scarce any thing that renders a man so useless as a pervers sticking to the same things in all times, because he has sometimes found them to have bin in season." *The History of the Royal Society,* &c. (ed. 1667), p. 335.

[5] Even in the first century, *obnoxius* was used to mean the same with *noxius,* 'hurtful, injurious'.

[6] "To the body diseases are infectious; to the mind are vices no lesse *obnoxious.*" Brathwait, *The English Gentleman,* &c., p. 140.

for 'reprehensible', by Dr. Fell, in the time of Charles II.; and I subjoin like instances from Dr. Donne,[1] Glanvill,[2]

Obnoxious here means 'likely to affect'. Compare the use of *subject* in the subjoined extract from Bp. Sprat: "A little knowledge is *subject* to make men headstrong, insolent, and untractable." *The History of the Royal Society*, &c., p. 429.

"But this interpretation will be found *obnoxious* to a double errour." George Ashwell, *Fides Apostolica* (1653), p. 216.

This *obnoxious to* bears the sense of 'chargeable with'.

"It may shun what is *obnoxious*, and seek after that which is profitable." R. White, Translation of *A Late Discourse*, &c. (ed. 1664), p. 89.

'Noxious' or 'injurious' is the signification of *obnoxious*, in this passage.

"This degrading the priesthood into a servile office takes off from that veneration which is due to the solemn mysteries of religion, and makes them look common and contemptible, by being administered by persons not sui juris, but *obnoxious* to the pleasure of those who receive them". Jeremy Collier, *Essays upon Several Moral Subjects*, Part I. (ed. 1703), pp. 205, 206.

In this place, *obnoxious* imports 'subservient'.

In the passages subjoined, *obnoxious* means, absolutely, 'liable', 'exposed', 'in peril'.

"'Tis just that all advantage that well can be should be afforded to the *obnoxious* party for his justification and deliverance." Barrow, *Works*, Vol. 1, p. 279.

"For these things are intolerably fastidious in conversation, and *obnoxious* to be charged with usurpation and iniquity." *Id.*, *ibid.*, Vol. 1, p. 394.

"So *obnoxious* are we to manifold necessities." *Id.*, *ibid.*, Vol. 1, p. 406. Also see p. 501.

"But the opinion of witches seems, to some, to accuse Providence, and to suggest, that it hath exposed innocents to the fury and malice of revengeful fiends, yea, and supposeth those most *obnoxious*, of whom we might most reasonably expect a more special care and protection," &c. Joseph Glanvill, *Essays*, &c. (1676), V., p. 13. Also see *Lux Orientalis* (ed. 1682), p. 8 (*bis*).

"The *obnoxious* strength and magnificence of imperial cities, and the less exposed and humbler abodes of private life, are equally subject to the general law which is carried into execution by the very nature of man." *Miss Carter's Letters to Mrs. Montagu*, Vol. 2, p. 80.

"But, from this his suspension (from the exercise of his jurisdiction), he was, in his own thoughts, buried; it reviving his *obnoxiousness* for his former casuall homicide." Fuller, *The Appeal*, &c., Part 3, p. 12.

Southey has "*obnoxious* to a rhyme"; Charles Lamb, "*obnoxious* to observation".

[1] "Of which [homicide] I perceive not any kinde to be more *obnoxious*, or indefensible, then that which is so common with our delinquents, to stand mute at the barre." *Biathanatos*, p. 123. Also see p. 163.

Donne is an earlier authority than Dr. Fell. He died in 1631.

[2] "'Tis fit I should give an account of an action so seemingly *obnoxious*." *Scepsis Scientifica*, *An Address*, &c.

"The longer I view the most likely of these hypotheses, the more liable and *obnoxious* I apprehend them." *Scire Tuum Nihil Est*, p. 50. And see pp. 54, 83. Also see Glanvill's *Plus Ultra*, *The Epistle Dedicatory* and p. 144: *Essays*, &c., II., p. 52; V., p. 19; VI., pp. 6, 45: *Lux Orientalis*, Preface (unpaged), and pp. 14, 126.

Here the sense is, much as at present, 'objectionable', 'exceptionable', 'objected to', &c. It is observable, further, that, in the second of these passages, Glanvill would deflect *liable* into a sense kindred to that of *obnoxious*.

Bishop Wilkins,[1] Henry More,[2] Dr. Bentley,[3] De Foe,[4] Bishop Warburton,[5] Samuel Richardson,[6] John Duncombe,[7] Henry Brooke,[8] Gibbon,[9] Burke,[10] Cowper,[11] Paley,[12] Porson,[13] and Godwin.[14] On the authority of Mr. White,

---

[1] "In respect of synonymous words, which make language tedious, and are, generally, superfluities, ... there is no particular language but what is very *obnoxious* in this kind." *An Essay towards a Real Character*, &c. (1668), p. 18.

[2] "Though Simon and the Gnosticks were thus grosly *obnoxious* in life and conversation," &c. *Mystery of Iniquity*, p. 453.

"By the favour of this ingenious writer, this hypothesis does not need any such *obnoxious* appendage as this", &c. *Annotations upon Lux Orientalis*, &c., p. 126. Also see p. 149.

"Their special *obnoxiousness* in that crime." *Ibid.*, p. 373.

An anonymous author wrote, in 1683: "When anybody prints an *obnoxious* pamphlet, they first send it to him by the penny-post." *The Loyal Observator*, p. 12.

[3] "There are some infidels, among us, that, ... to avoid the odious name of atheists, would shelter and screen themselves under a new one of deists, which is not quite so *obnoxious*." *Works*, Vol. 3, p. 4.

[4] "He [Satan] has a great many other names and surnames which he might be known by, of a less *obnoxious* import than that of Devil, the Destroyer, &c." *The Political History of the Devil*, p. 38.

[5] "And, as this was the case, I endeavoured, in these *obnoxious* words, to shew," &c. *A Selection*, &c., p. 172.

[6] "As from a man of quality, and the son of a nobleman who had been *obnoxious* to ministers," &c. *Correspondence*, Vol. 6, p. 172. Also see *Clarissa Harlowe* (ed. 1811), Vol. 1, p. 129: *Sir Charles Grandison*, Vol. 3, p. 187; Vol. 5, p. 244.

[7] "The uses of the *obnoxious* garments were allowed to be many." *Connoisseur*, No. 62.

[8] "I purposely avoided appearing in her presence, lest the sight of one so *obnoxious* should add to her distemper." *The Fool of Quality*, Vol. 2, p. 255. Also see Vol. 3, p. 257.

[9] "My grandfather could not expect to be treated with more lenity than his companions. His Tory principles and connexions rendered him *obnoxious* to the ruling powers: his name is reported in a suspicious secret;" &c. *Memoirs of my Life and Writings*.

[10] "No complaisance to our court, or to our age, can make me believe nature to be so changed but that public liberty will be, among us, as among our ancestors, *obnoxious* to some person or other." *Thoughts on the Cause of the Present Discontents*.

A dozen more instances might be added from Burke.

[11] "I subjoin the lines with which I mean to supersede the *obnoxious* ones in Expostulation." "Those *obnoxious* doctrines at which the world is so apt to be angry." *Works*, Vol. 4, pp. 161, 200.

[12] "*Obnoxious* principles in politics." *Moral Philosophy*, Book 6, Ch. 10. Many other instances might be adduced from Paley.

[13] "I now come to your arguments against these *obnoxious* versions." *Letters to Mr. Archdeacon Travis*, p. 159.

[14] "The people of England have assiduously been excited to declare their loyalty, and to mark every man as *obnoxious*, who is not ready to sign the shibboleth of the Constitution." *An Enquiry concerning Political Justice*, Preface, pp. x., xi.

the word has come to be employed, in its more modern acceptation, "particularly by those who do not know exactly what it does mean". Among these ignoramuses, besides those already mentioned, have been Coleridge,[1] Wordsworth,[2] Southey,[3] Sydney Smith,[4] Lord Macaulay,[5] and Dr. Newman.[6]

The connexion, by a comical oversight, being "unless a man is a crown-prince, or other important public functionary", Mr. White counsels that he should "reject, disown, refuse, or condemn what he does not like, but not *repudiate* it, unless he expects to cause shame, or to suffer it, in consequence of his action".

It is by no means certain, however, that the Latin original of *repudiate* has any etymological relationship to *pudere* and *pudor*. The primary meaning of *repudiare* seems to be 'reject', 'renounce';[7] and *repudiatio* and *repudiator* have no classical acceptations but those of 'rejection' and 'rejecter'. Bentley tells us that atheists "*repudiate* all title to the kingdom of Heaven".[8] Those

---

1 *Essays on His Own Times*, p. 471.

2 "Yet, while the partisans of the French are thus guarded, not a word is said to protect the loyal Portuguese, whose fidelity to their country and their prince must have rendered them *obnoxious* to the French army." *Concerning the Relations*, &c., p. 86. Also see p. 77; and *A Letter to a Friend of Robert Burns*, &c., p. 3.

3 A certain office, he writes, "is, always and justly, *obnoxious*, when performed by an informer". *Essays, Moral and Political*, Vol. 2, p. 227. Also see p. 416. In Southey's *Life of Wesley* I find this use of *obnoxious* no fewer than twelve times.

4 "The officers commanding corps, finding that no steps were taken to remove the *obnoxious* insinuations," &c. *Works*, p. 189.

5 "Both were personally *obnoxious* to the Court." *Essay on Sir James Mackintosh*. "The *obnoxious* minister." *Essay on the Earl of Chatham*. "*Obnoxious* persons were insulted and hustled." *History*, Chapter 10.

6 "The Stationarii were appointed, in various places and stations, to inform against *obnoxious* persons." *Fleury's Ecclesiastical History*, Vol. 1, p. 325, note k.

7 So the French say "*répudier* une succession"; and the Italians, "*repudiare* un' eredità".

8 *Works*, Vol. 3, p. 13. At p. 221 of the same volume, Bentley writes of "*repudiating* at once the whole authority of revelation," &c.

"He is defended by the like practice of other writers who, being Dorians born, *repudiated* their vernacular idiom for that of the Athenians." *Ibid.*, Vol. 1, p. 359.

"To *repudiate* was, formerly, to put away what disgraced us; it now signifies (in America, at least) to reject the claims of justice and honour." *Last Fruit off an Old Tree*, p. 102.

It is strange that a scholar of Landor's calibre could let such an assertion as

who assert a right to *repudiate* their debts will, let us hope, fare like the atheists. At the same time, as to their English, they are not to be numbered among the transgressors.[1]

"*Restive* means 'standing stubbornly still', not 'frisky', as some people seem to think it does. A *restive* horse is a horse that balks; but horses that are *restless* are frequently called *restive*. *Restiveness*, however, is one sign of rebellion in horses. Thus, Dryden (quoted by Johnson):

'The pampered colt will discipline disdain,
Impatient of the lash, and *restiff* to the rein.'

---

to our old sense of *repudiate* escape him, and, especially, that he could have forgotten Bentley's employment of the verb in his Dissertation on the Letters of Phalaris, just adduced, and the Hon. Charles Boyle's criticism thereon.

Gibbon, in his *Memoirs of my Life and Writings*, says: "After my return to England, I continued the same practice, without any affectation, or design of *repudiating* (as Dr. Bentley would say) my vernacular idiom."

The dormitancy—sit venia verbo—of great classical scholars is, not unfrequently, surprising. Mr. De Quincey, having used the adjective *veterinary*, comments thus on it: "By the way, whence comes this odd-looking word? The word *veterana* I have met with, in monkish writers, to express 'domesticated quadrupeds'; and, evidently, from that word must have originated the word *veterinary*. But the question is still but one step removed: for how came *veterana* by that acceptation in rural economy?" *Works*, Vol. 14, p. 377, foot-note.

Not to appeal to the astonishing school-boy whom Lord Macaulay so often summoned, to the confusion of those that knew less than himself about hole-and-corner facts, one may be allowed to wonder that Mr. De Quincey was not familiar with the ancient *veterinarius* and *veterinus*, and was not aware of the derivation of them which has very plausiby been conjectured.

[1] "I shall shew the convincing evidence of this truth, ... which hath been so universally received by them who have *repudiated* or reformed all that they could find any fault with, after a most severe examination," &c. George Ashwell, *Fides Apostolica* (1653), p. 101. Also see p. 274.

Repudiate means, here, as in the passages to follow, simply 'reject' or 'put away', irrespectively of a sense of shame or disgrace. It points rather to pure aversion.

"And all reasoning that is not supported so ought to be *repudiated*, or, at least, suspected to be illegitimate." R. White, Translation of *A Late Discourse*, &c. (ed. 1664), p. 75.

"I detest it, I hate it, I *repudiate* it." Sterne, *Tristram Shandy*, Vol. 8, Ch. 11.

"If they had rejected it upon examination, they would have written about it; they would have given their reasons. Whereas, what men *repudiate* upon the strength of some prefixed persuasion," &c. Paley, *Evidences of Christianity*, Part 3, Chapter 4.

"They stoutly *repudiate* those notions of a Priesthood which the Succession doctrine really involves in it." Dr. Arnold, *Life and Correspondence*, p. 544. Also see p. 562. See, further, Dr. Arnold's *Miscellaneous Works*, p. 471.

"In *repudiating* metaphysics, M. Comte did not interdict himself from analysing or criticizing any of the abstract conceptions of the mind." Mr. J. S. Mill, *Auguste Comte and Positivism*, p. 15. Also see p. 65.

Hence a misapprehension, by which those who did not understand the word were led to a complete reversion of meaning."

Very few instances, I apprehend, can be produced, from our literature, of that use of *restive* which Mr. White thinks to be the only right one; and most of the extracts which the dictionaries cite under the word illustrate a signification of *restive*, the sole signification it has long borne, which the lexicographers do not distinctly recognize.[1] Even the passage which Mr. White takes from Dr. Johnson is nothing to his purpose. Among old meanings of *restive* are 'disposed to draw back',[2] and, much more rarely, 'quiescent,' 'sluggish'.[3] The ordinary sense of the word has always been 'unruly', 'intractable', 'refractory'. Proofs are subjoined from Lord Brooke,[4] Dr. Featly,[5] Fuller,[6] Milton,[7] Jeremy Collier,[8] Samuel Richard-

---

[1] Dr. Johnson's definitions are: "1. Unwilling to stir; resolute against going forward; obstinate; stubborn. 2. Being at rest; being less in motion."

[2] *Resty*, as applied to a horse, is defined, by Miege, "qui recule au lieu d'avancer". Dr. Johnson says, less correctly: "It is originally used of an horse that, though not wearied, will not be driven forward." *Rétif* is thus defined by M. Littré: "Se dit d'un cheval ou autre bête de monture qui refuse d'obéir à celui qui le monte ou qui le conduit."

[3] "What would the ear serve for, if the air were not suitably disposed—made neither too thick nor too thin, neither too *resty* nor too fleeting, but—in a due consistency, and capable of moderate undulations distinguishable thereby?" Barrow, *Works*, Vol. 2, p. 92.

"Both fancy and judgment are commonly comprehended under the name of wit, which seemeth to be a tenuity and agility of spirits, contrary to that *restiness* of the spirits supposed in those that are dull." Hobbes, *Works*, Vol. 4, p. 56.

[4] "Since I have shewed you, by reason, that obedience is just and necessary; by example, that it is possible; be not *restive* in their weake stubburnnesse that will either keepe or lose all." *Certaine Learned and Elegant Workes*, &c. (1633), p. 286.

Still older is the following: "As a man . . delivereth over his horses—which, because they have been in many skirmishes, are become *resty*, furious, and untractable,—to the yomen of his horses," &c. T. Bowes (?), *The French Academie* (ed. 1589), Vol. 1, p. 320.

[5] "Where mettle colts or *restie* jades are to be broken, he that holdeth not a streight raine, and maketh not use of a strong curbe, may be cast out of the saddle." *Abel Redevivus*, p. 487.

[6] "Like *resty* horses, we go the worse for the beating, if God bless not afflictions unto us." *The Holy State and the Profane State*, p. 187.

[7] "In state, perhaps, they [chaplains] may be listed among the upper serving-men of some great household, and be admitted to some such place as may style them the sewers or the yeomen-ushers of devotion, where the master is too *resty*, or too rich, to say his own prayers, or to bless his own table." *Eikonoklastes*, Chapter 24.

[8] "Socrates had as *restive* a constitution as his neighbours, and yet reclaim'd

son,[1] Burke,[2] Coleridge,[3] Mr. De Quincey,[4] and Landor.[5] As concerns a horse, however he resists an attempt to keep him quiet, he shows himself *restive.*[6]

It must be superfluous to dwell any longer on such particulars as have hitherto engaged us. In the domain of generalities, at the same time, it is instructive to see what Mr. White has to give us, by way of maxims.

"There is a misuse of words which can be justified by no authority, however great, by no usage, however general." [7]

But what considerations avail to override universal usage? They are known, we are given to understand, by the intuition proper to philological illuminati.

"When a word, a phrase, or an idiom is found in use both in common speech and in the writings of educated men, we may be almost sure that there is good reason for the usage. But cultivated and well-meaning people sometimes take a scunner against

---

it, all by the strength of his philosophy." *Essays upon Several Moral Subjects*, Part III., p. 77.

[1] "My aunt has held him in, till her arms ached. O, the dear *restiff* man!" *Sir Charles Grandison*, Vol. 6, p. 341.

We have had *restive*, *restiff*, and *resty;* and we have had *mastie*, *mastive*, and *mastiff*. *Resty* is marked, by Dr. Webster's editors, as "obsolete". I have often heard it, from Englishmen and Englishwomen, in conversation, especially in the form *rusty*. "But they paraded the street, and watched the yard till dusk, when its proprietor ran *rusty*, and turned them out." Mr. Charles Reade, *Hard Cash* (ed. 1863), Vol. 3, p. 199. This corruption, as Dr. Johnson shows, is not modern.

[2] "Everything you say of the *restive* and stubborn temper of America recoils upon yourself." *Correspondence*, Vol. 4, p. 484.

[3] "But Truth, I remember, is reported to have already lost her front teeth . . . . by barking too close at the heels of the *restive* fashion: a second blow might leave her blind, as well as toothless." *Notes and Lectures upon Shakespeare*, &c., Vol. 2, p. 339.

[4] "Mr. Waterton . . . . publicly mounted and rode in top-boots a savage old crocodile, that was *restive* and very impertinent, but all to no purpose. The crocodile jibbed and tried to kick, but vainly." *Works*, Vol. 4, p. 307, foot-note. Also see Vol. 3, p. 184; Vol. 5, p. 63; Vol. 6, p. 308; Vol. 11, p. 124; Vol. 13, p. 293; Vol. 14, pp. 369, 372.

[5] "Oft, when the Muses would be festive,
Unruly Pegasus runs *restive.*"
Heroic Idyls, p. 188.

[6] "A *restive* horse, &c. From the verb to *resist*. Resistive: res'stive: restive." Mr. H. Fox Talbot, *English Etymologies*, p. 199.

This is anti-historical; *restive* being from the Old French *restif*, connected with the Low Latin *restivus*. Yet it is possible that our *restive* has taken a tinge from association in idea with *resist*.

[7] P. 24. This passage has been quoted before. Mr. White himself almost repeats it, at p. 253.

some particular word or phrase, ... and they flout it pitilessly, and think, in their hearts, that it is the great blemish upon the speech of the day." [1]

I have but a vague apprehension what a *scunner* [2] is; but I strongly suspect it to be the very thing that has animated Mr. White in his numerous raids against allowable phraseology.

"There is no surer way to a weak, poor, artificial style than the sitting in judgment upon the use of words and phrases of spontaneous growth, which are not at variance with reason, and which have long been used by all classes of speakers for centuries. A man who uses language as Sampson, the valiant retainer of the Capulet, bit his thumb, only when he has the law on his side, will soon come to write like an attorney drawing a law-paper." [3]

There is a sound about this which suggests the evangel of freedom. But who is to sift the right from the wrong for us? Mr. White, of all men, we are taught to infer.

"If Walter Scott, fifty years ago, and Henry Fielding, a hundred and twenty-five, called beauties and sensible girls *first-rate*, surely I, in these days, may, with calm indifference to consequences, so call the journal in which, and the critic by whom, I am reproved. But I had, of course, no thought of these precedents, when I wrote, and should have used the phrase without scruple, even were I sure that it had never been used before." [4]

Mr. White being a law to himself, of course his critics were guilty of the grossest presumption.[5]

---

[1] P. 257.

[2] The author's scholiasts will fall short of their function, if they forget to throw light on this vocable. It may be Scotch by origin.

In the same paragraph where Mr. White terms the very expressive and felicitous metaphor *presidential campaign* "a blatant Americanism", he writes of "*army-bumming* bombast". After twenty-six years' absence from America, I read Mr. White's book at some disadvantage, as regards fully appreciating its vernacular delicacies. But would it not have been better, in a work of serious import, to avoid local and ephemeral slang?

His minor Americanisms—such as *aside*, for 'apart', p. 20; *belittling*, for 'disparaging', p. 219; and *bestead with*, for 'beset with' or 'infested with', p. 238,—have the good fortune of being interpretable by help of the context.

"People", he tells us, at p. 220, "do not learn good English, or good manners, by verbal instruction received after adolescence. Every man is like the Apostle Peter, in one respect, that his tongue bewrays him." These words bear every note of having been prompted by an irretentive conscience.

[3] Pp. 125, 126.

[4] P. 258.

[5] Ships, cart-horses, scholars, and many other gross objects are properly

"Any man has the right to use a word, especially a word of such natural growth and so well rooted as *juxtapose*, for the first time; else we should be poorly off for language."[1]

Only woe to the man so authorized, if Mr. White's opinion does not chance to coincide with his own.

Reduced to its simplest expression, the principle on which Mr. White criticizes our language is whim. The very fundamentals of true philology he has still to acquire. Of illustrative authority for words and their senses he knows but very little;[2] and that little, for the most part, he invokes for his support, or disdainfully sets aside, solely in obedience to caprice.

> Non amo te, Sabidi, nec possum dicere quare;
> Hoc tantum possum dicere, non amo te.

---

enough called *first-rate;* and so teas and silks are properly enough called *first-chop;* and there is not much to choose between the taste which would apply the former to a lady and that which would thus apply the latter. The point in question is not one of good English, or bad; and Mr. White runs no risk of indictment or excommunication, if he thinks good to grovel. But the fitness of things is a matter which people of culture claim to take cognizance of; and autocratic bluster is not likely to work its extinction.

That Mr. White is ready to defer to Sir Walter Scott as, independently, an authority for recent English is significant. Both Fielding and Sir Walter have written "had *spoke*", and have used *plenty* as an adjective. Mr. White must, therefore, recommend "calm indifference to consequences", on the part of any one that is minded to do likewise.

[1] P. 259. But how could Mr. White bring himself to write "poorly *off*"? For is not *off*, here, an adverb become an adjective? I refer to what he says of *ill*. *Vide supra*, p. 83.

Where it pleases Mr. White, both length and authority of usage are admitted as arguments. Thus, in treating of *reliable*, he urges that "the usage in question has been too short and too unauthoritative to have any weight". I shall only mention, at present, that *reliable* was used by Coleridge, and in print, in 1800.

[2] "For two centuries and a half, since the time when *King Lear* was written, and our revised translation of the Bible made, the English language has suffered little change, either by loss or gain. . . . To his [Shakespeare's] vocabulary they [English-speaking men] have added little except words which are names for new things. The language has not sensibly improved, nor has it deteriorated." P. 25.

Such could not be the opinion of one who had given serious thought to the development of English in modern times. Among our verbs, adjectives, and adverbs, those which were unknown to Shakespeare may be reckoned by thousands.

Shakespeare's vocabulary is, substantially, that of his contemporaries, who cannot be supposed to have been unintelligible to one another; and we find it remarked, in 1698, that "some who wrote at the beginning of this century are not now easily understood." Hon. Charles Boyle, *Dr. Bentley's Dissertations . . . . Examined*, p. 69.

Nor are his notions of verbal genetics at all less superficial than his acquaintance with practical precedents. Accordingly, as has been abundantly evidenced, where his adjudications do not contravene approved usage, they are almost certain to clash with etymology or with analogy. Marvellously is his fortune like that of Saint Matthew's lunatic: "for ofttimes he falleth into the fire, and oft into the water." To execute successfully such a book as he has miscarried in attempting, it is by no means enough to trust to memory, and to pore upon dictionaries, glossaries, and concordances. To say anything new, that is also true, about words and meanings of recent origin, one must not merely read widely, but must take copious notes on what one reads; and the indispensable preparation for discussions such as he has essayed, Mr. White would appear to have well nigh entirely neglected. And this is not all. Neither has he explored our literature with the eye of a philologist, nor does he give proof of any but very commonplace and incogitant excursions beyond the limits of his mother-tongue. In a word, he could never be mistaken, except by the very ill-informed, for anything but what he is. Of his volume he himself tells us: "Scholars and philologists need not be told that it is not addressed to them; but neither is it written for the unintelligent and entirely uninstructed."[1] From the detail and earnestness with

[1] Preface, p. 7. Mr. White, as might have been expected, has been perstringed by sundry of his better-informed readers; and his style of self-defence speaks amply for itself. For instance, he wrote that *risible* "is not formed from the verb *rideo*, 'to laugh' (although, of course, derived from it), but from the noun *risum*, 'a laugh', or 'laughter'." P. 418. Charged, for this, with a two-fold display of ignorance, after asserting that adjectives in *-bilis* "are sometimes made from nouns", he has recourse to trite figures of bad rhetoric, hylactismus and oncethmus, and goes on to say: "*Risibilis* (which, I have heard it whispered, is not the best Latin) is, of course, the counterpart of *risible*, or was when I went to school; and, as to *risum*, at that time I met with the following line in a Latin author, Horace, who was held up to me as a poet of some repute:

Spectatum admissi *risum* teneatis, amici?

and this *risum* I translated, without reproach, 'laughter'; parsing it as the accusative case or objective form of *risus*." P. 422.

On the very lowest of all motives, bare expediency, it is better, when one has been convicted of blundering, to own it frankly and fully, like an honest man. Mr. White wishes, of course, to produce conviction in his own favour; and, since he addresses this vindication of himself, if to any purpose, to a degree of inapprehension peculiar to a very ill-informed class of judges, it is no wonder that he warns off "scholars and philologists" from his lucubrations.

which it dwells on such distinctions as those between *lie* and *lay*, *sit* and *set*, one would, rather, conclude that it was

---

If he knows of any adjectives in *-bilis* that are "made from nouns", he knows more than the grammarians; and his deducing *risibilis* from the substantive *risum* is precisely as if he were to deduce *mode* from *modum*. Whatever was the Latinity of his earlier years, no doubt he mistook, in his riper years, *risum* for a nominative. And why bring forward the fact that *risibilis* "is not the best Latin", and throw himself into a jaunty attitude, and indulge in recondite quotation? Dust of this sort will find no eyes but those of the illiterate. Real answer he has none; and he does not even use effectually "the flat hand of rhetoric, which rather gives pats than blows", as Fuller has it. The word *risibilis* is analogical; though, even if it were not, the fact would in no way aid Mr. White towards showing that he had not committed an error of crass ignorance; and his academical friends, at sight of his subterfuge and mystification, must be moved to laughter, quite as much as the good people were whom he resuscitates out of Horace. It is altogether credible, especially from what follows, that he could hardly afford to adopt the tone of the rollicking old rimester who sings:

"What though brieves, too, be made longos?
What though vowels be diphthongos?
What though graves become acute, too?
What though accents become mute, too?
What though freely, fully, plainly,
I've broke Priscian's forehead mainly?"
Barnabæ Itinerarium (ed. 1818), p. 181.

For, at p. 285, he quotes from Catullus:

"Tua nunc opera meæ pullæ [*sic*]
Flendo turgiduli rubent ocelli,"

which he translates: "Now the pretty swollen eyes of my mistress redden with weeping thy doings." If Mr. White had learnt a little Latin prosody, it would have benefited his Latin syntax; but, evidently, the mystery of Roman hendecasyllabics was not included in the curriculum of his juvenile studies. Otherwise, he would have perceived that *opera* is not from *opus*, and that it is not an accusative. Thus much and more has already been pointed out by one of Mr. White's critics.

Dryden, what between "the tumult of his imagination and the multitude of his ideas",—see the *Rambler*, No. 31,—once slipped into the Hibernianism of writing:

"I follow fate, which does too fast pursue";

and his defence, when the absurdity was pointed out, might, for its impotent inconclusiveness, have served Mr. White as a model; as might, again, the shuffling of Hobbes, when it was observed that he had misunderstood and misused the word *potentiality*.

"Now, men may love their enemies, and do good to them that hate them; but men will never love their critics, or do anything but evil to them that ridicule them. As to criticism men are unwise; but, in regard to ridicule, they have some reason. Accusation of crime is trifling in comparison." *Life and Genius of Shakespeare*, p. 89.

Thus Mr. White on one of the "dangerous classes", and a weapon of theirs which, sometimes, they wield quite warrantably; and the tone is not that of fiat justitia et ruant cœli. Those who treat this gentleman irreverently are precautioned as to what they may look for. Their lot is not a pleasant one, certainly; and yet it might be greatly worse. Let them, for instance, picture to themselves the misery of being audibly and orthoepically designated by the

designed for "the unintelligent and entirely uninstructed", more particularly,—persons of the class of Steele's two ladies who begged him to explain the difference between *circumcision* and *predestination*.[1] But why such an unmistakable shrinking from the inspection of "scholars and philologists"? Instruction, though ever so humble and elementary, ought to be correct, as far as it goes; and, if Mr. White had been quite confident of his position, it would scarcely have occurred to him to deprecate the notice of the learned. His labours are, consequently, to be understood as being tentative, experimental; and his game of hazard has not ended altogether prosperously.

One of ten British writers, belonging to the last century and to this, whom Mr. White holds up as models for their English, is Mr. Thackeray; and, among Mr. White's American models, are Mr. Washington Irving and Mr. Hawthorne.[2] Elsewhere,[3] Mr. Thackeray and Mr. Hawthorne are especially singled out for the correctness of their English; and we are interrogated: "While Hawthorne lived,—and his grave is not yet as green as his memory,—was there a British writer who used with greater purity, or more plastic power, the language that we brought with us from the old home?"[4] Now, on the score of the copiousness with which Mr. Irving and Mr. Thackeray exemplify bad English, I have long been accustomed, when in quest of that disagreeable article, to confine myself to their pages.[5] Mr. Hawthorne is better; and yet,

---

plain English of *asini;* the epithet crushingly delivered with "the full, free, unconscious utterance of the broad *ah* sound of *a*", that "surest indication, in speech, of social culture which began at the cradle". *Vide supra*, p. 50.

[1] See the *Tatler*, No. 232.

[2] P. 55.

[3] "Now, that man, if he had been speaking to his wife, would have called out 'Sairy Ann, the carriage has come', and have rivalled Thackeray or Hawthorne in the correctness of his English." P. 36.

[4] P. 46. At p. 78, Mr. Hawthorne's English is once more an object of laudation.

[5] As to Mr. Thackeray, a single one of his works will serve my turn amply. Let it be *Vanity Fair*, my copy of which was printed in 1856.

But, first, I will quote him for words, uses thereof, and phrases, which Mr. White himself, aright or amiss, expressly declares against.

"The parson and the Baronet talk about the pigs, and the poachers, and the county business, in the most *affable* manner, and without quarrelling in their cups, I believe." P. 78. See *Words and Their Uses*, p. 86.

"While these delicacies *were being transacted* below," &c. P. 212. Also see pp. 89, 105, 152.

in turning over *Our Old Home* for a few minutes, I have lighted upon *bug* for *insect, demean* for *disgrace, parties* for

---

"Our friend returned to London, to *commence* those avocations," &c. P. 382. *Vide supra*, p. 38, text and note [1].

"She cast about among her little ornaments, to see *could she sell* anything to procure the desired novelties?" P. 389. See *Words and Their Uses*, p. 52.

"But his face, when he heard it, showed an amazement which was very different *to* that look of sentimental wonder," &c. Pp. 182, 183. See *Words and Their Uses*, p. 48.

"Lady Jane . . . ran to her husband's room, *directly* she heard Mrs. Rawdon Crawley was closeted there." P. 461. See *Words and Their Uses*, p. 186.

"There was such a jubilee and sense of relief, in all Miss Crawley's house, as the company of persons assembled there had not *experienced* for many a week before." P. 203. Also see pp. 394, 576.

"Yet she felt a horror and uneasiness in their presence, and longed to *fly*." P. 577. See *Words and Their Uses*, p. 115.

"There were Irish gentlemen, with the most dashing whiskers and *jewellery*." P. 520.

"He kept a journal of his voyage, and noted elaborately the defects or excellencies of the various inns at which he put up, and of the wines and dishes of which he *partook*." P. 522. Also see p. 497, for two instances. See *Words and Their Uses*, p. 143.

"Some few score of years afterwards, when all the *parties* represented are grown old," &c. P. 188. Also see p. 278. See *Words and Their Uses*, p. 143.

"Amelia, too, might have *recovered the shock* of losing him." P. 185. See *Words and Their Uses*, p. 52.

"Georgy *stopped* away from school." P. 515. See *Words and Their Uses*, p. 197.

"Amelia . . . . flung herself into George Osborne's arms with all her soul, to the astonishment of everybody who *witnessed* that ebullition of sentiment." P. 89. Also see p. 373. See *Words and Their Uses*, p. 175.

I now instance specimens of English which, like most of those just given, it would be imprudent to recommend for imitation.

"One of the domestics was *affected* to his especial service, attended him at his toilette," &c. P. 474.

"Thus an *almost* reconciliation was brought about," &c. P. 313.

"As they had been in the habit of being together *any time* these fifteen years," &c. P. 42. Also see pp. 125, 366, 461, 491, 520, 569.

"Even the O'Dowd was silent and subdued, after Becky's brilliant *apparition*," &c. P. 233.

"The fact is, he owed more money *at* London than at Paris." P. 305.

"What has *come* of Major Dobbin, whose cab was always hankering about her premises?" P. 320.

"It was, of course, Mrs. Sedley's opinion that her son would *demean* himself by a marriage with an artist's daughter." P. 40. Also see p. 408.

"He walked all the way home very *dismally*, and dined alone with Briggs." P. 437.

"*Everybody* had been dull, but had been kind in *their* way." P. 355.

"She cried *fit* to break her heart." P. 117. Also see pp. 239, 532.

"Think of *him* writing such a hand." P. 494.

"Perhaps the Doctor's *lady* had good reason for her jealousy." P. 324.

persons, *plenty* for *plentiful*, and "he had named his two children, one *for* Her Majesty, and the other *for* Prince Albert." Dr. O. W. Holmes is, also, selected from what some one calls "the illustrious family of the Issimi", as a writer "whose English, as well as whose thought, merits the attention and admiration of his readers".[1] In *The Autocrat of the Breakfast-table*, I find, however, "step out here into the grass *back of* the church", "swinging *back* and forward", "*belittle*",[2] "I remember a young

---

"He was *only good enough to be* a fairy prince." P. 91.

"He could see, with a fatal *perspicuity*, that there was no place there for him." P. 299.

"He, I *promise*, did not decline the obsequious invitation," &c. P. 497.

"A few score yards down . . . . is a little modest back door, which you would not *remark* from that of any of the other stables." P. 391.

"*Neither* of us *ride* so light as we did," &c. P. 457.

"'By Jove, how they made you cry out!' said Joe, caught by the *ridicule* of the circumstance," &c. P. 21.

"Well, let us see . . . . if, some day or *the* other, I cannot show Miss Amelia my real superiority over her." Pp. 68, 69.

"The *Major's* windows, *who* had lodgings opposite, under the Prime Minister, were always open," &c. P. 533.

"This *young person* . . . . loved, with all her heart, the young officer," &c. P. 90. Also see p. 101.

Add *avocation* for 'vocation', *demise* for simple 'death', *servitude* for 'domestic service', and *mutual tears*, with the Scotticisms *clavers* and *vilipend*. Nor is our language improved by the substantives *appropinquity*, *divagation*, *otiosity*, by the adjective *melancholious*, or by the verbs *discord*, *olden*, *prodigate*, *streel*.

[1] P. 252.

[2] Somehow, I meet with this word, at least every week, in New York newspapers, notwithstanding the note, by Dr. Webster's editors: "Rare in America". Besides this, many of my countrymen stand up for it very stiffly. Hereon I differ from them; and I think it can be shown why they ought to give it the cold shoulder.

First, though Bishop Sanderson has used *beguilty*, and though *bedismal* and *begaudy* have got into print, I am not aware that we have ever had, in our language, a single accepted verb in which *be-* was prefixed to an adjective that had not previously become, itself, a verb. So it was with *belate*, whence *belated*. *Little* is no verb; and *belittle* is indefensible by any established analogy.

Secondly, *belittle*, as defined by Dr. Webster's editors, signifies "to make little or less in a moral sense; to lower in character". If *little* always referred to moral estimate or level, *belittle* would be slightly less bad than it is. At present, to those who are unversed in American literature, it is often inevitably a puzzle what is intended by it.

Thirdly, it has no visible chance of becoming English; and, as the more critical writers of America, like all those of Great Britain, feel no need of it, the sooner it is abandoned to the incurably vulgar, the better.

No less bad, from an analogical point of view, is Lord Macaulay's reflexive verb *bemean*, for *demean*, as certain writers, generally correct in their diction, once used it, and as Mr. Thackeray and Lord Lytton have used it in our own

wife who had to part *with* her husband for a time", "an opinion *predicated* on the supposition", &c.; and, in *The Professor at the Breakfast-table*, "*dasher*",[1] "I trust him as much as I should do, if he felt *of* the outside of my strong-box", "her hair looked *strangely*", "the spiritualists have some pretty strong instincts to *pry*[2] over", &c. &c.[3]

---

time. *Bemean*, I am aware, for 'make mean', was in print in 1688: and it ought to have been left quiet in its grave. Mr. Charles Reade uses it in *Griffith Gaunt*.

It is very thoughtless in the lexicographers to quote Shakespeare as authority for the *demean* connected with *mean*. Still, Archdeacon Todd has been able to adduce a seventeenth-century instance of it.

"He [Ridley] was translated to the bishoprike of London, wherein how he *bemeaned* himselfe shall hereafter be related." Thus, according to what is printed, writes Gataker, in *Abel Redevivus*, p. 193. I surmise, however, what Fuller calls a *prelal* error; for, at pp. 196, 214, 404, 459, 527, Gataker, intending, as there, 'comport', uses *demean*.

The ancient source of *demean* is unascertained. That we took the word from the French, all are agreed. But whence came *demener* and *mener*? Some deduce *mener* from the classical *minari*, through the Low Latin *minare*; Mr. Wedgwood connects it with *manus*. M. Burguy, who pronounces for *minari*, thinks that *mine*, 'air', 'manner',—the parent of our *mien*, another word of disputed etymology,—is from the same original. See his *Grammaire de la langue d'oïl*, Vol. III., p. 244.

Nether, and accordantly with analogy, has been used, as a verb, in the sense which some still give to *demean*. "*Nethered*, brought low, debased." Verstegan, *Restitution*, &c., p. 244.

[1] In English, *splash-board*; in Scotch, *dash-board*.

[2] For *prize*. The barbarism *pry* still lingers among the common people in East Anglia; but, elsewhere in England, it is as unintelligible as if it were Choctaw.

[3] Among American writers, Mr. W. D. Howells, we are bid to believe, shows an "unobtrusive and seemingly unconscious mastery of idiomatic English." "Directly" for 'as soon as', "white-*teethed*", "*on* the street", and "to *settle* for the wine", occurring in his *Italian Journeys*, are, indeed, reprobated; but, adds Mr. White: "These four slips are notable, as being all that I remarked, in reading *Italian Journeys* thoroughly and carefully. There have been very few books, if any, published on either side of the water, that would not furnish more, as well as greater, opportunities to a carping critic."

Mr. White must be a careless reader. In the work in question I find "aggravate" for 'provoke', p. 66; "Cupids escaping from cages, and *being sold* from them", p. 284; "Englishry" and "shrubbery", in the acceptations of 'English people' and 'collection of shrubs', respectively, pp. 165, 31; the verb "experience", pp. 22, 164, 174, 239; "trying to *fly* their bargain", p. 128; "reliable", p. 181; "witness" for 'see', pp. 24, 97, 196, 238; "I wonder *did Petrarch walk* often down this road from his house just above", p. 220. All these expressions Mr. White decrees, in his *Words and Their Uses*, to be reprehensible.

I find, also, "everybody is *anecdoted*", p. 170; "attributive" for 'putative', pp. 202, 268; "back and forth", p. 71; "he . . . *besought* to take us, as a special favour", p. 183; "deboshed" for 'debauched', p. 254; "develop" for 'reveal', p. 72; "in view of" for 'in consideration of', pp.

A very long list would be the result, if I were to specify even a tithe of the solecisms sanctioned by writers whom Mr. White extols as exemplary. On the other hand, it

---

80, 270; "muletress", a malformation, p. 120; "under *way*" for 'under *weigh*', p. 271; "unrivaledest", p. 253. A few sentences and parts of sentences may be added.

"Their landlord, their porter, their driver, and their boatmen pillage them with the same impunity *that* they rob an Inglese." P. 12.

"If *one* use *his* eyes half as much as *his* wonder," &c. P. 18.

"But, though we were ten days in Naples, I *only saw* one quarrel," &c. P. 78.

"We *were masters* to *have taken* the steamer, instead of the diligence, at Civita Vecchia." P. 182.

"We entered the lagoon, and found it a nest of fortresses *one with another*." P. 273.

"There were large placards everywhere posted, *notifying the people* that it was forbidden," &c. P. 297.

"From these [notes] I think it no *dereliction* to quote verbatim." P. 309. "Dereliction" is here used for 'breach of promise'.

"This is one of the *things* that *makes* a single hour of travel worth whole years of historic study," &c. P. 316.

Out of a great number of solecisms in an earlier book by Mr. Howells, *Venetian Life*, I select "accredit" for 'credit', p. 93; "each" for 'every', pp. 13, 97, 146; "G. is not good *for* reading and writing", p. 104; "as this excuse *gives out*, she ceases to respond to his ring *at all*", p. 106; "*multiple* forms", p. 188; "*mutual* friends" for '*common* friends', p. 309; "the lowest style of any *other*", p. 257; "signalize" for 'testify', p. 240; "sparsity", p. 330; "stomach" for 'sicken', an obsolete Italianism, pp. 76, 307; "thereafter" for 'thenceforward', 'for the future', 'subsequently'. pp. 238, 289. "He told us he was a Constantinopolitan, and that, in six months, he *would* complete his collegiate course, when he *would* return to his native city, and take employment in the service of the Turkish Government." P. 193. "When I gave him a soldo, he gave me a blessing which I *would* be ashamed to take, in the United States, for half a dollar". P. 308. These last sentences are worthy of Mr. White himself, as evincing "mastery of idiom". *Vide supra*, pp. 48, 49. Among expressions which Mr. White would especially condemn, is—not to mention "*bountiful* largess", p. 16,—*beggary*, for 'beggars', p. 262. *Vide supra*, p. 85.

Nor does Mr. Howells's English improve much; as witness a few extracts from his *Suburban Sketches*, published last year:

"He said he *allowed* [*i. e.*, consented] to work it out." P. 58.

"Think of *him* making me stop the other day." P. 146.

"How it could have come *of* that colourlessness . . . . was a question." P. 93.

"It seemed long *till* that foolish voice was stilled." P. 206. Is this barbarous use of *till* peculiar to the West? It occurs in *Venetian Life*, also, pp. 96, 114. I know it only as an Irishism, in modern times.

Then we find "cloggist", p. 210; "a *cycle* since", p. 104; "discommode", p. 24; "populatory", p. 57; "our *regrettable* climate," p. 17. And we still have, in spite of Mr. White, the Scotch "*upon* a street", "*on* a street", pp. 16, 38, 175, 182; "*experience* relief", p. 54; *witness*, for 'see', p. 64; and *was being made*, p. 198.

To say truth, among American writers of rising fame whose English is noticeably bad, Mr. Howells stands somewhat eminent.

has been seen how many fashions of speech which he rejects and ridicules are practically warranted by Lord Macaulay, a writer whom, at least as an affirmative authority,—for much which he tacitly stamps as unpermissible other good judges account permissible,—all agree, with Mr. White, in holding in high esteem. Briefly, instead of a knowledge of precedents, and of the history of words, Mr. White's chief capital consists of gratuitous personal prejudices; and, what between these, an utter defect of scholarly tact and instinct, a sanguine persuasion of his own faultlessness,[1] and the most uncompromising intolerance, his criticisms and judgments are what might be anticipated. If even a small fraction of his arraignments were well-grounded, no one, within several hundred years, can have done more than approximate to writing good English;[2] and composition, to himself, must be perpetual torture. Justice forbids that he should be summed up as anything but a word-fancier. Philology, with Mr. White, as political economy, with Mr. Ruskin, seems to rank as one of the fine-arts.

To reason from a man's practice as a writer to his antecedents as a heedful reader is, surely, equitable. Mr. White is so good as to let us know, in one of his autobiographic digressions, that, dating from a certain point in his career, "*Thereafter* I studied English, indeed, but only in the works of its great masters, and, unconsciously, in the speech of daily companions who spoke it with remarkable but spontaneous excellence."[3] Now, where, one is curious

---

[1] "I might have crucified most of my critics upon crosses made out of their own heads." P. 394.

This reminds one of the Ernulphian vein of the two doctors in Mr. Longfellow's *Golden Legend*.

> "*Doctor Serafino*. May the Lord have mercy on your position!
> You wretched, wrangling culler of herbs!
> *Doctor Cherubino*. May he send your soul to eternal perdition,
> For your treatise on the Irregular Verbs!"

[2] The days of King James's editors of the Bible satisfy his conditions of that right English which requires *brake*, *gat*, and *spake*; but those same days give us *digged* and *shined*, which he abhors; the verb *execute*, which, used of a criminal, "produces sheer nonsense"; and the adjective *ill*, for which "there is no defence and no excuse, except the contamination of bad example". All days, moreover, since there has been such a thing as English, have given us 'the sun *sets*', which he calmly spurns at, as "quite indefensible". The only possible inference, from these and similar premises, is, that we lucky mortals have been born just in the fulness of time, to see our language exemplified in its perfection—by Mr. White.

[3] P. 276.

to ascertain, did he get permission from the "great masters" to use *thereafter* as an adverb of time, correlative to *hereafter*?[1] Is this use of the word to be met with in the Bible,[2] in Shakespeare, in Milton, or in a single modern British author of notable value for the purity of his language? It occurs in Robert of Gloucester, and in Spenser, I am aware; but their successors have almost wholly relinquished it to the Scotch and other outsiders to whom the English of England is more or less a foreign tongue. Again, when Mr. White writes "she hated

---

[1] *Thenceforth* or *thenceforward* is the word Mr. White should have chosen. In old writers we find *then after*, also. See Bernard's *Terence in English* (1588), p. 249 (ed. 1607); a saying attributed to Sir Thomas More, among the *Wise Speeches* in Camden's *Remains;* and Bp. Sanderson's *Sermons*, Vol. 2, p. 253.

"Whereupon, Drake, though a poor private man, *hereafter* undertook to revenge himself on so mighty a monarch." *The Holy State and the Profane State*, p. 124. Fuller must have had a very strong aversion to *thereafter*, or he would not have wrested *hereafter* to mean 'after *that*'.

Again: "Never he was seen heartily, if at all, to laugh *hereafter*." *The Appeal of Injured Innocence*, Part 3, p. 12.

Mr. De Quincey, in Vol. 7, pp. 89, 90, asserts, with his usual exaggerativeness, that *thereafter*, for 'after that', is "not even intelligible in England". He goes on to say: "*Thereafter*, in pure vernacular English, bears a totally different sense. . . . . The objections are overwhelming to the Scottish use of the word; first, because, already in Scotland, it is a barbarism, transplanted from the filthy vocabulary of attorneys, locally called writers; secondly, because, in England, it is not even intelligible, and, what is worse still, sure to be misintelligible." Further on, it is scouted as a property of "leguleian barbarism".

Certainly, *thereafter*, in any sense whatever, is not a word in everyday English use; but any Englishman, on hearing it from another, except in a quotation from some old or quaint author, would at once take 'after that' to be intended by it. This, of course, Mr. De Quincey knew perfectly well; and, looking to his fertility of resource, one would suppose that, with less than half the spleen and splutter he has expended on *thereafter*, he might have contrived to impart to his readers the valuable information that he had acquainted himself with its obsolete signification, 'accordingly'.

In literature, it has not often been used in this sense, I believe, during the last century and a half. "That, madam, is *thereafter* as they be." Gay, *Beggar's Opera*, Act 2, Scene 1.

Thereafter, for *thenceforward*, or *after that*, is common enough in the English of Scotchmen and Irishmen. See, for some oldish instances, Lithgow, *The Totall Discourse*, &c., pp. 84, 149, 202, 273, 346, 347, 375, 407, 432, 448; the Bishop of Kilmore, in *Abel Redevivus*, pp. 59, 62 (*ter*); and extracts in Glanvill's *Sadducismus Triumphatus*, pp. 391, 393.

Even more justifiable, on one ground, is the vulgar *nohow*. *Thereafter* mates with *hereafter* only; but *nohow* is in analogy with both *anyhow* and *somehow*. *Thereby*, for 'near to that', is just as accepted English as Mr. White's *thereafter*.

[2] See p. 17, note [2], near the end.

him *all the same*",[1] meaning 'nevertheless', he as little adheres, in this Scotticism bred out of bad French, as in his *scunner* and *bumming*,[2] to the phraseology of the "great masters".[3] Referring to America, "That there are journalists in this country", he says, "whose English is

[1] P. 184. [2] *Vide supra*, p. 99, text and note [2].

[3] Let us also look at some passages in Mr. White's *Life and Genius of Shakespeare*.

"It is impossible that he could have written it without thinking of his own experience; the more, *that* the seeming lad to whom it is addressed is about his years," &c. Pp. 53, 54.

This savours of the north of the Tweed.

"Ralph, however, like most disappointed lovers, *concludes* to live." P. 387.

Conclude means 'come to a conclusion', in one sense of the phrase, that which gives to *conclusion* the meaning of 'inference'. *Conclusion*, in this phrase, also signifies 'resolution'; but *conclude*, as equivalent to the phrase when it attaches this sense to *conclusion*, has long ceased to be English.

In pp. 31, 114, 149, is the very common Americanism "*aside* from", for '*apart* from'; in pp. 19, 227, 351, "belittle".

Either and *neither*, for 'any one' and 'none', are not English. "That he wrote the plays which bear his name we know; but, except by inference, we do not know the years in which they were written, or even that in which *either* of them was first performed." P. 4. "Peasant, yeoman, artisan, tradesman, and gentleman could then be distinguished from each other almost as far as they could be seen. Except in cases of unusual audacity, *neither* presumed to wear the dress of his betters." P. 155. Also see pp. 185, 402.

Amid (p. 1), *ere* (p. 91), the substantive *hate* (p. 1), and the verb *joy* (pp. 258, 262) are out of place in prose. *Indefinity* (p. 228) is not a pretty word; *play-wright* (pp. 268, 384) should scarcely be used, save in derision; *so absolutely* (pp. 394, 402) and *so perennial* (p. 400) can hardly be justified. *In this regard* (p. 299), *in that regard* (pp. 72, 396), are affected. And so is *mayhap* (pp. 16, 83, 138, 191). If this, why not an occasional *belike*, *eftsoons*, *muchwhat*, or *whilom*?

"At school, Shakespeare acquired some knowledge of Latin and of Greek. For not only does Ben Jonson tell us that he had *a little* of the former, and *less* of the latter, but," &c. P. 31. "These stories grate upon our feelings with a discord as much harsher than that which disturbs us when we hear of Addison suing poor Steele for £100, as Shakespeare lives in our hearts the lovelier as well as the greater man than Addison." P. 146. "Davenant was, morally, a poor creature; and, in this, he only *did his kind*." P. 158. "When he [Aufidius] first saw his wedded mistress *bestride* his threshold." P. 258. "It is probable that not *one* in ten of the English plays written before the time of Shakespeare *have* escaped destruction." P. 315. "But the comely dame, who seems to be *a tall woman of her hands*," &c. P. 388. The imagination, as one reads this group of extracts, fastens, involuntarily, and in spite of Shakespeare, on the straddling pose of Mrs. Aufidius. Tastes will differ, I know, as to the archaisms here instanced.

Thus fares it with our Zoïlus,—

Ἄλλων ἰατρὸς, αὐτὸς ἕλκεσι βρύων.

But, for fear of becoming tedious, I desist, after noting that Mr. White's *bestead* and *conclude*, now unenglish, though once otherwise, have escaped all the lexicographers.

irreproachable, no one competent to speak upon this subject will deny."[1] This decision, considering who passes it, is not necessarily irreversible.

An exhaustive critique on *Words and Their Uses* would demand as much space as the work itself occupies. Only here and there a statement, out of those which, on a careful reading of it, I scored for remark, has been subjected to animadversion. The last third of the book, and, especially, the chapter entitled *The Grammarless Tongue*,[2] often degenerates, with oases of rationality, into downright silliness.[3] Of Mr. White, save as a literator, I know no-

---

[1] P. 56.

[2] Dr. Johnson is reported to have said: "Foreign idioms . . . have been decried as dangerous; and the critics daily object to me my Latinisms, which, they say, alter the character of our language. But it is, seriously, my opinion, that every language must be servilely formed after the model of some one of the ancient, if we wish to give durability to our works." *Monthly Magazine* (1800), Vol. 9, p. 150.

"Another will say, it [our language] wanteth grammer. Nay, truly it hath that prayse, that it wanteth not grammer: for grammer it might have, but it needes it not; beeing so easie, of it selfe, and so voyd of those cumbersome differences of cases, genders, moodes, and tenses, which, I think, was a peece of the Tower of Babilon's curse, that a man should be put to schoole to learne his mother-tongue." Sir Philip Sidney, *An Apologie for Poetrie* (ed. 1868), p. 70.

If none but the so-called classical languages can have grammar, or, in other words, be grammatical, then, as to English, it follows, either that,—seeing what, in spite of its ungrammaticalness, it has got to be,—it is too noble a thing to endure grammatical shackles, or else that, however refined it may become, there is something, in its original nature, which exempts it from the contemplation of grammar. This alternative we are forced to by taking 'grammar' in the absurdly limited acceptation of Sir Philip Sidney and Mr. White. But Mr. White, by the very fact of his eulogizing, on all practicable occasions, correct vernacular concord and regimen, that is to say, the main essentials of grammar, reduces English to the same category with Latin and Greek. Nay, to go beyond concord and regimen, he espouses, in theory, as we have seen in his treatment of *convene* and *resurrect*, the principle of explicit servility advocated by Dr. Johnson. Such is his consistency, with his contention that our tongue is "grammarless".

[3] Mr. White's proficiency in English grammar has been rendered extremely doubtful by an admirable series of papers which appeared, soon after his book came out, in *The College Courant*, published at New Haven. No other review of *Words and Their Uses* has reached me; and much that I have said may have been said before by others.

Whatever contempt for English grammars may possess Mr. White, he would not do amiss to be accurate about them. Ben Jonson and Milton, he remarks, "both were misled, very naturally, into writing an English Grammar". P. 344. As Ben Jonson lived till 1637, and as Milton was born in 1608, the two might have cooperated in such an undertaking. But history is silent on this point; and it is also silent as to Milton's having written an English Grammar by himself. Did Mr. White ever see the performance? Again, at

thing; and I am willing to believe that he is endowed with every civic and social virtue. Yet non omnia possumus omnes. Success in one department of letters, a department congenial to his proper aptitude, has emboldened him to venture his cunning in another department, and one in which he is totally incapable of distinguishing himself. Research, logicalness, circumspection, subtilty, all these are things which it would be flattery to predicate of him. His assumption of judicial assessorship, as a critic of English, is, therefore, to borrow a word from Hazlitt, altogether ultra-crepidarian. Coleridge says, of some one, that, after turning over a few books, he "puts on the seven-league boots of self-opinion, and strides, at once, from an illustrator into a supreme judge"; and the type of adventurer thus delineated is realized by Mr. White, even as, in water, face answereth to face. The evidences are sown broadcast, that, for his reputed knowledge of our language, he has become the cynosure of an admiring coterie, in which he rules as umpire and oracle; and, as a critic before the world, to what extent, if unchecked, may he not propagate, among the unthinking and uninformed, the contagion of his numberless crotchets and crudities![1]

---

p. 180, he gives a quotation from "Graham's" *Word Gossip*. The book quoted is by Mr. Blackley. At pp. 128 and 200, the interesting old letter-writer Howell figures as "Howells". These are specimens of a heedlessness which is, plainly, habitual.

[1] It is amusing to see the imperial air with which he enounces his behests to applicants for his manuduction. When, however, they presume to doubt and boggle, it is "Really, I hope my friends will not misapprehend me, when I say that it is, generally, safe to assume that the court knows a little law." P. 395.

Something like a panic, it seems, has been occasioned, by the meteoric appearance of Mr. White, among the proprietors of divers old-fashioned school-books, which sundry of his admirers have petitioned him to supersede by something sounder. "Why, even already the priests of the present idols have begun to denounce a certain pestilent fellow, and their craftsmen to cry 'Great is Diana of the Ephesians'." P. 400.

A new grammar Mr. White appears to have projected with some seriousness; and he drops hints of a new dictionary, likewise. To think of the good they might effect, and of the glory they might gain him, warms the very cockles of his heart. "It would be delightful to believe that the next generation would rise up and call me blessed." In a much lower key, he adds: "but I am, of necessity, much more interested in the question, whether the present generation would rise up and put its hand in its pocket, to pay me for my labour." P. 397. Very fortunately, little harm is to be apprehended, even though the present generation were not to subserve the beatification of Mr. White, by utilizing his pedagogic aspirations.

To expose baseless pretensions has not, however, been my motive, in my dealings with this gentleman. Regard for the interests of sound learning and common sense has, alone, induced this cursory examination of some of his statements and deductions. His teachings, as being, in the main, grossly erroneous, deserved to be counteracted; and to counteract them was impracticable without evincing, simultaneously, that, whatever be his forte, philology is his foible. Were his shortcomings the result of sloth only, such is my preference for impersonality, that

> Non partis studiis agimur, sed sumpsimus arma
> Consiliis inimica tuis, ignavia fallax

might serve as the motto of my strictures on him. It would have been much more agreeable to me, if his book had been anonymous; and, besides, his mistakes, with those of Mr. De Quincey and the rest, would never have moved me to write in a polemic spirit, except that, in an essay not aiming at anything like method or completeness, they were serviceable as introductions to a few discursive hints on the necessity, in order to just philological conclusions, of patient inquiry, cautious reflection, and dispassionate judgment.

ADDITIONS.

P. 4, notes, l. 15. Fuller, in *The Holy State and the Profane State*, pp. 4, 422, makes *corpse* plural; but, at p. 347, he writes "*a* dying corpse". In his *Abel Redevivus*, p. 19, we read "his corpes *were* burnt". "Their corps *were* burnt." Dr. Featly, *ibid.*, p. 478. "His corps *was*," &c. Gataker, *ibid.*, p. 407.

"It is curious to observe how the English Catholics of the seventeenth century wrote English like men who habitually spoke French. *Corps* is sometimes used for 'the living body'." Southey, *Omniana*, Vol. 2, p. 131.

This remark has, certainly, very little warrant. As to *corps*, since it denoted, as it now denotes, a specific collection of living bodies, to make it import a single living body was to alter its use but slightly. Verstegan gives it a wider latitude of meaning than that now attached to it. "The main *corps* and body of the realm . . . . hath still consisted of the ancient English-Saxon people," &c. *Restitution*, &c., p. 203. "The *corps* or body of the realm." *Ibid.*, p. 308. At p. 250, Verstegan writes, as many authors of his century write, and not, to their consciousness, tautologically, "a *dead* corps". And so Heylin: *A Full Relation*, &c., p. 373. Lithgow, a sufficiently exacerbated Protestant for Southey himself, without either Gallicizing or Scotticizing, has: "The rememberance of these sweet seasoned songs . . . . did recreate my fatigated *corps* with many sugred suppositions." *The Totall Discourse*, &c., p. 69.

P. 18, note 5. In evidence that Dr. Johnson, as a lexicographer, recognized *individual* in the character of a substantive, we have the fact that his second definition of the substantive *particular* is: "*Individual;* private person." Again, his third definition of *person* is: "*Individual;* man or woman."

P. 30, notes, l. 15. Disliking to make an assertion of which the proof is not at once producible, I regret that the existence, in English literature, of *musicianer*, a word I have again and again seen in old books, must here be left unestablished. It is used, however, by the Scotchman Lithgow, in *The Totall Discourse*, &c., p. 98.

P. 32, l. 13. On looking over my notes, I see that I can allege numerous other instances of the verb *experience*, scattered through the literature of four centuries. A couple of quotations are subjoined, with a few references.

"Your soul will then *experience* the most terrible fears, if you do not recover yourself into the fold and family of God's Church." Southwell, *Poetical Works* (ed. Mr. W. B. Turnbull, 1856), Preface, p. lvi.

Southwell was judicially murdered in 1595, at the early age of three and thirty. It is worth noting that the poetical remains of this saintly man were first collected, more than two centuries and a half after his death, by a person who, like himself, fell a victim to Protestant bigotry.

"All the active power and vigour of the mind, our faculties of reason, imagination, and will, are the wonderful result of this mutual occurse, this pulsion and repercussion of atoms; just as we *experience* it in the flint and the steel"; &c. Bentley, *Works*, Vol. 3, p. 42. Also see p. 67 of the same volume.

Two sermons delivered in 1692 are here referred to.

See, further, Henry More, *Annotations upon Lux Orientalis*, &c., pp. 17, 29, 39 (*bis*), 51, 52, 53, 81, 123: Bishop Warburton, *A Selection*, &c., pp. 27, 372, 431: John Wilkes, *The North Briton*, Numbers 6, 14, 17, 28, 39, 42: Horace Walpole, *The Castle of Otranto*, chapters 2 and 4: William Godwin, *The Enquirer* (1797), pp. 31, 62, 68, 163, 189, 230, 272, 273, 313, 419: Mrs. Godwin, *Posthumous Works* (1798), Vol. 1, p. 144; Vol. 2, p. 139; Vol. 3, p. 102: Sydney Smith, *Works*, pp. 17 (*bis*), 24, 27, 36, 57, 58, 69, 74, 83, 88, 119, 154, 182, 186, 195, 244, 253, 291, &c. &c.

P. 53, note 1. Since p. 53 was printed off, I have seen it announced that a new edition of *Words and Their Uses* is in preparation. I will, therefore, here mention, that, to the authorities for expressions like *is being built*, which I formerly adduced, I can now add Shelley, Mrs. Shelley, Dr. Arnold, Dr. Newman, Mr. Ruskin, and the Rev. Charles Kingsley. The last name does not, perhaps, deserve recording. Still less, at all events, do the names of Lord Lytton, Mr. Thackeray, Mr. Dickens, and Mr. Froude, as concerns a point of language.

P. 55, ll. 19, 20. Some verbs in *-en* which have been proposed have failed of being adopted. Two such are here exemplified.

"To conclude, as your wild fancy (if you were surpriz'd of any) is now rectifi'd, your coolenesse *heatned*, your coynesse banished," &c. Brathwait, *The English Gentleman*, &c., p. 357.

"For his great heart, instead of fainting and subsiding, rose and *biggened* in proportion to any growing danger that threatened him." Sir Richard Steele, *The Christian Hero*, p. 45 (ed. 1711).

P. 70, notes, l. 4. *Redevivus* is the word in Fuller's own title.

P. 94, ll. 1, 2. "If you examine a man that has been well disciplined by philosophy, you 'l find . . . . . no selfish, no *obnoxious* and absconding practices." Jeremy Collier, *The Emperor Marcus Antoninus his Conversation with Himself*, &c. (1701), p. 35.

"Any the most *obnoxious* argument." Bishop Hurd, *Moral and Political Dialogues* (ed. 1760), p. 15. Also, see pp. 31, 42.

AUTHORS, ETC.

*** The letter f., where attached to the number of a page, is intended to denote the pages immediately following.

WORDS AND PHRASES.

*** Of the terms referred to as illustrations, the more common are not here indexed.

WORKS BY THE WRITER OF THIS CRITIQUE.

SANSKRIT.

The Âtmabodha, with its Commentary, and the Tattvabodha. Pp. 29 and 9. Mirzapore: 1852.

The Sânkhyapravachana, with its Commentary. Pp. 66, 233, and 44. Calcutta: 1856.

The Sûryasiddhânta, with its Commentary. Pp. 4, 388, and 13. Calcutta: 1859.

The Vâsavadattâ, with its Commentary. Pp. 56, 300, and 6. Calcutta: 1859.

The Sânkhyasâra. Pp. 51 and 48. Calcutta: 1862.

The Dasarûpa, with its Commentary, and four chapters of the Nâṭyaśâstra. Pp. 39 and 241. Calcutta: 1865.

HINDÎ.

The Tarkasangraha, translated into Hindî from the Sanskrit and English. Pp. 24 and 48. Allahabad: 1850.

The Siddhântasangraha, translated into Hindî from the Sanskrit and English. Pp. 7, 72, and 96. Agra: 1855.

Hindî Reader. Pp. 19 and 184, quarto. Hertford: 1870.

MISCELLANEOUS.

Lectures on the Nyâya Philosophy, Sanskrit and English. Revised edition. Pp. 14 and 80. Benares: 1852.

The Râjanîti, in the Braj Bhâshâ Language. Pp. 7, 167, 10, and 14. Allahabad: 1854.

Classical Selections. Pp. 2 and 256. Agra: 1855.

A Contribution towards an Index to the Bibliography of the Indian Philosophical Systems. Pp. 2 and 236. Calcutta: 1859.

A Rational Refutation of the Hindu Philosophical Systems, translated from the Hindî and Sanskrit. Pp. 10 and 284. Calcutta: 1862.

Ane Compendious and Breve Tractate, &c., By William Lauder (1556). Pp. 11 and 39. London: 1864. Second edition, revised, pp. 11 and 43. London: 1869.

Sir David Lyndesay's Works. Four Parts. Pp. 548. London: 1866—1869.

Benares, Ancient and Medieval: a Monograph. Pp. 23. Hertford: 1868.

The Vishnupurâṇa, Annotated Edition of Professor H. H. Wilson's Translation. Five Volumes. Pp. 140 and 200; 343; 343; 347; 392. London: 1864—1870.

IN PREPARATION.

Modern English.

JOHN CHILDS AND SON, PRINTERS, BUNGAY.

www.ingramcontent.com/pod-product-compliance
Lightning Source LLC
LaVergne TN
LVHW021420110826
845150LV00007B/2003

* 9 7 8 1 4 2 5 5 0 9 2 0 0 *